CONTENTS

FOREWORD

Whatever views are held on the nature and content of secondary education, there is general agreement that the ethical dimension of the school curriculum is of the utmost importance. Yet this aspect of education has not always been given the attention it merits either in debates about the curriculum or in in-service provision for teachers. This book is, therefore, very timely, and it gives me particular pleasure to welcome its publication by the University College of Swansea Faculty of Education, under the editorship of Dr. Lionel Ward. The collection of papers is based on a conference for headteachers and staff specialising in personal, social, religious and moral education, organised in November 1981 by the Faculty of Education and sponsored by the Welsh Office Education Department. Dr. Ward, as conference leader, was successful in attracting some of the most distinguished figures in the field in Britain as the main speakers. The Faculty is most grateful to all who responded to his invitation to participate in the conference, as well as to the other contributors to the book, including two from overseas. I am sure that the papers will be of wide interest, and serve as a stimulus to further thinking and discussion on the topics which they cover.

Maurice Chazan
Dean, University College of
Swansea Faculty of Education.

CONTRIBUTORS

Gerald H. Gardiner

Head of Religious Studies
Burleigh Community College
Loughborough

Brian Gates

Head of Religious Studies and Social Ethics
S. Martin's College, Lancaster

Paul H. Hirst

Professor of Education
University of Cambridge

Jean Holm

Principal Lecturer in Religious Studies
Homerton College
Cambridge

Lawrence Kohlberg

Professor of Education
Harvard University, U.S.A.

Denis Lawton

Deputy Director
University of London Institute of Education

Peter McPhail

Former Director
Schools Council Moral Education Project

P.W. Musgrave

Professor of Education
Monash University, Australia

Richard Pring

Professor of Education
Exeter University

Lionel O. Ward

Lecturer in Education
University College of Swansea

John Wilson

Lecturer in Educational Studies
University of Oxford

Derek Wright

Professor of Education
University of Leicester

PREFACE

This book is intended to be a contribution to the current debate on the content of the school curriculum, at the same time to offer practical help to those who wish to do more than just engage in that debate. Discussion at a national level, especially as it has been carried on in Department of Education and Science documents, has identified eight areas of the child's experience[1]. For many of those concerned with the curriculum the most profoundly important area of experience for the child and for society is the ethical one, the area usually associated with personal, social, religious and moral education. The lack of established knowledge in this field referred to by R. S. Peters[2] is not, of course, recitified here, but what is offered is a wide variety of perspectives on the problem by some of the most distinguished authorities concerned.

The intensity of the general debate on the curriculum, the background to which is discussed in Chapter 1, has not entirely submerged discussion of the ethical dimension of the school curriculum. Indeed, the leading figure in the investigation of the developmental sequencing of morality outlines recent work in Chapter 2, and in Chapter 3 concern for moral education is shown to be international. Some of the complexity of the subject is revealed in Chapter 4, especially the relationship of religion to morals in the present state school. The school operates within a social context, as Chapter 5 outlines, and the relative influences of school, family and community are hard to determine. For many the desirable aim is the development of the morally autonomous child, which is the subject of Chapter 6. The teaching process itself cannot be devoid of moral assumptions and implications and this is discussed in Chapter 7. The first steps of the moral educator are traced in Chapter 8, and succeeding chapters broaden the discussion to practical suggestions for personal, social, religious and moral education. Chapter 9 describes the work being done in personal and social education, Chapter 10 shows how the established role of religious education in the curriculum can assist ethical development and Chapter 11 gives guidance for those concerned for emphasising the school as community, especially through assemblies. Finally, in Chapter 12, a teacher experienced in the field describes the programmes and materials available in moral education.

As Peter McPhail has recently argued, moral education in some form is a task which cannot be avoided, and we had better do it well[3]. The new spirit that has entered discussions of moral education is illustrated uniquely in the most recent work of R. M. Hare. In 'The Language of Morals', published thirty years ago, he was concerned almost entirely with the search for meaning, and later he considered, in 'Freedom and Reason', the grounds for moral decision-making. His recently-published book 'Moral Thinking' reflects his sense of urgency about the present, his hope that philosophers might help resolve practical problems, his concern that rational thinking and talking will avoid conflict and catastrophe[4]. Hare distinguishes two levels of moral thinking: the critical level, which we employ when deciding the best principles to adopt for resolving moral conflicts; and the initiative level, which represents our 'gut reaction' to a particular moral crisis. His attempts to demonstrate how the right principles worked out at the critical level can be used to cultivate the best heartfelt dispositions at the initiative level, are helpful to the arguments expressed in this book that moral responses are the work of the whole personality. It is this whole personality with which schools have to be concerned.

The editor acknowledges gratefully the assistance of the Dean of the University College of Swansea Faculty of Education in writing the Foreword and the Faculty of Education, with its secretary Mr. R. E. George, for sponsoring the book. Chapters 1, 6, 7, 8, 9, 10, 11 and 12 are based on lectures given at a conference sponsored jointly by the Welsh Office Education Department and the Faculty of Education. Chapters 2, 3, 4 and 5 were contributed specifically to this book and Chapters 2, 4 and 7 embody work originally published elsewhere and revised for this book by their authors. The editor expresses his grateful thanks to all these contributors. Mrs. Katrina Guntrip undertook the typing with encouraging enthusiasm and unfailing expertise. Finally, I acknowledge the encouragement and constructive criticisms of my wife in preparing the manuscript and her help in reading the proofs.

Notes

1 Department of Education and Science, Curriculum 11 - 16. Working Papers by H.M. Inspectorate, H.M.S.O., 1978; Curriculum 11 - 16. A Review of Progress, H.M.S.O., 1981.

2 Peters, R.S., Moral Development and Moral Education, Allen and Unwin, 1981.

3 McPhail, P., Social and Moral Education, Blackwell, 1981.

4 Hare, R.M., The Language of Morals, Oxford University Press, 1952; Hare, R.M., Freedom and Reason, Oxford University Press, 1963; Hare, R.M., Moral Thinking, Oxford University Press, 1982.

Chapter 1

CULTURAL ANALYSIS AND EDUCATION: PAST AND PRESENT

Denis Lawton

The tradition of thinking about education in terms of a selection from the culture of a society goes back at least as far as Matthew Arnold, in England. His position was particularly interesting, if occasionally confused, because as a poet he made a contribution to "high" culture; as a literary critic he became involved in social analysis as well as the purely aesthetic, and as an HMI he was directly involved in attacking the 1862 Revised Code narrow curriculum, pointing out the need for a much richer, more open curriculum for all social classes. John Ruskin, William Morris and, more recently, Raymond Williams have continued in the tradition of seeing education as a means of transmitting culture rather than simply preparing the young for work and "citizenship".

In recent years that particular conflict of views has, to some extent, been reflected in documents produced by Her Majesty's Inspectors and the Department of Education and Science. The HMI have adopted a broader cultural approach in Curriculum 11 - 16 and A View of the Curriculum, and also in the Primary and Secondary Surveys, whilst the DES are still very much in the "Gradgrind" camp - especially in Framework for a School Curriculum and The School Curriculum.

The DES documents are interesting for another reason which Robert Dearden has seized upon in a recent paper[1]. Much has been made since the Great Debate of 1976 to 1977 of the desirability of "balance" and "coherence" in the curriculum. I will not attempt to summarise Dearden's argument here, but simply say that the use of both words tends to beg important questions and probably raised more problems than it solves. The balanced curriculum metaphor is, however, a particularly interesting one. Presumably, either "balance" is regarded as a good quality in its own right, or the idea of a balanced curriculum is parasitic upon the idea of a balanced diet. A useful analogy up to a point, perhaps, but if we use it we should use it carefully. One of the problems is that the idea of a balanced diet rests on well-established scientific data in the field of nutrition about vitamins, proteins, carbohydrates, minerals, etc. There is general agreement about these components of a balanced diet, but there is no such agreement about the ingredients of a balanced curriculum. The DES writers of Framework for a School Curriculum and other documents assumed this agreement without justification. We cannot progress to a consideration of balance without certain prior commitments about what ought to be balanced. Yet this is just what the curriculum amateurs at the DES did in 1980, when they assumed (in Framework) that balance is a question of balancing subjects - hence 10% English, 10% mathematics, etc.

In curriculum, we have not yet even identified the ingredients let alone started quantifying them. The DES curriculum cooks are not yet at the Marie Antoinette stage of saying "No bread? Let them eat cake!"; they are saying quite firmly "Give them bread, but not the cake!". I am sure they are not yet at the stage of the Scottish naval surgeon, James Lind, who in 1752 showed that sailors could avoid suffering from scurvy at sea if they ate oranges and lemons - although he did not know why. To change the metaphor, the DES authors are pretending to be brain surgeons when they are only pox doctors' clerks.

Although we are still a long way away from a consensus position about curriculum components, a good deal of work has been done from a philosophical point of view about the necessary "prior commitments" - for example, R.S. Peters has helped considerably to clarify the concept of education, and Hirst and others have gone some way towards clarifying the structure of knowledge in the educational context[2]. But philosophers such as Hirst have readily accepted that the leap from abstract discussions of educational principles and the structure of knowledge to curriculum planning is a considerable one, which should be bridged by social considerations as well as the purely epistemological ones. Planning education is not simply a problem of sub-dividing knowledge.

In the past, I have attempted to deal with some aspects of this problem by defining curriculum as a selection from the culture, and then making the selection partly on the basis of philosophical principles and partly by considering "the needs of society" (if you allow me to beg that enormous question for just a moment). Perhaps it would be more acceptable to talk of the needs of an individual living in a particular society or simply of social trends or cultural variables.

The advantage of a two stage process of selection is that it avoids the danger of sociological determinism - if we operated (made the selection from the culture) without any attention being paid to principles or universals outside that particular society, then schools and teachers would become mere state functionaries just reflecting the needs of society. If that were the case, then we would have "correspondence theory" working without any obstacles. But if teachers do not simply pass on automatically the knowledge, skills and values, but make some kind of selection, then they must make that selection according to certain other principles which over-ride particular social pressures. Teachers in Nazi Germany, for example, who wished to resist the instructions to inculcate anti-semitism and other aspects of Nazi propaganda, had to have access to certain ethical principles which they felt over-rode the demands upon them as teachers in a particular society at a particular point in time.

What we need to work on, therefore, is an examination of cultural universals, including any values which would help guide the educational selection process in any one society. Education is concerned with certain abstract values such as Truth, even if it is not always easy to pronounce upon "the truth"; education must be concerned with Beauty even if we find if difficult to decide on why something is more beautiful than something else.

Some sociologists and anthropologists such as Ruth Benedict have emphasized the differences between societies; others such as Clyde Kluckhohn have stressed the essential cultural similarities[3]. A process of cultural analysis applied to education and curriculum planning will require a three-stage process: first, it will be necessary to identify a limited number of "cultural universals" i.e., those characteristics which all human beings appear to have in common in all societies; second, to examine one particular society in the light of those cultural universals; and, finally, to examine educational implications of that process of cultural analysis.

I would suggest that we need to look at seven cultural universals:

1. social structure
2. communication
3. rationality
4. technology
5. morality system
6. belief system
7. aesthetic criteria and practices.

These are universals in the sense that no society exists without any one of them and probably no society could exist without them. These are the institutions, values and beliefs which have to be transmitted to the next generation.

But associated with these seven are universals of another kind, i.e., values which are good in themselves irrespective of any particular society.

We are all relativists now, but there are limits - i.e., there are values and criteria by which particular practices in any society can be judged. (If so, what are they?).

1. Social structure

All societies, by definition, have some kind of social structure - a system of defining relationships within the society as a whole. Kinship, status, role, duty and obligation, are the key social concepts which not only exist in every society, but have to be passed on to the next generation if that society is to survive. In some societies, the social structure is relatively simple and taken for granted; in others, the social structure is highly complex, open to debate and possibly to change.

The social structure will be closely related to economic and technological factors: for example, when Western European societies were largely rural and agricultural, the dominant factor in the social structure was the relationship between those who possessed and those who did not possess land. We sometimes find it convenient to refer to this as feudalism. As trade and industry developed, land became less important than the possession or non-possession of capital. The social structure now became much more concerned with individuals and the ownership or non- ownership of the means of production than of land (although there is, of course, a good deal of overlap). Although social structure will be seen as one of the key features of cultural universals then, the variety of systems of social structure is enormous and change does take place over time.

2. Communication

In all societies, human beings communicate with each other. One of the major differences between man and other animals is the power of language. Where communication is entirely by means of spoken language most, if not all, of the learning required is informal, perhaps even unconscious (children are unaware that they are learning a language, and parents unaware that they are teaching when they provide a speech model). In some societies, speech is not the only form of communication: American Indians have sign languages and smoke signals, for example; other societies have developed various kinds of writing; most societies have visual symbols of some importance. These "non-speech" forms of communication are often acquired less "automatically" or "naturally" than speech, and usually some kind of teaching process is involved.

3. Rationality

Language and communication pre-suppose some form of rationality. If individuals communicate, certain basic rules of meaning and logic must apply. Much discussion has taken place about the cultural universals and cultural variables as regards forms of rationality[4]. In any society, the act of communication takes for granted certain basic rules or principles about meaning and truth. Chomsky's work has emphasized the essential similarity in deep structure between all human languages[5]. A basic human logic exists despite cultural variables in such matters as language and also on attitudes to magic, science or religion.

4. Technology

Human beings everywhere attempt to lessen domination by the environment and sometimes to control the environment. Early man developed tools to build shelter from the climate, to kill animals for food, later to produce food by agriculture. Human beings everywhere are technologists in the sense of being tool makers and tool users, and they make progress by passing on their developing technology, with improvements, to the next generation. Learning to use and to improve tools is everywhere a feature of cultural life.

In some societies, technology is comparatively simple, and differences in access to the technology are almost non-existent; in modern industrial societies, however, no one person could possibly be skilled in all aspects of technology, so specialisation and then inequality of access become problems for that society. In complex industrial societies, the difficulty is not simply one of transmitting knowledge and skills, but of "allocating" or selecting some individuals for certain kinds of learning, and allocating others for different learning processes. Selection takes place within the educational process and perhaps contaminates the educational purposes.

5. <u>Morality system</u>

Another characteristic that all human beings have in common is that they have a sense of "the moral"; all societies have a code of ethics, distinguishing between right and wrong behaviour. What is regarded as right or inappropriate will vary enormously from one society to another, but there is no culture where human beings live in a community without a sense of "mores" or ethics. In some societies, the moral code is unitary and taken for granted; in other societies, value pluralism exists, and the problem of socialising the young is then much more difficult: total agreement will be lacking, but some kind of rules will need to be transmitted for society to survive.

6. <u>Belief system</u>

Closely connected with the morality system is the local ideology or belief system. In some societies the moral code will be backed up by, and closely related to, religious dogma or divine revelation or myths about the origin of the community; in other societies those links have become weakened, or the prevailing belief system will be entirely secular - perhaps a belief in science or rationalism where "man is the measure of all things". In that kind of society, the problem of educating the young and passing on a belief system will be much more difficult, not least because the young will be encouraged to question and criticise rather than simply learn and accept.

7. Aesthetic criteria and practices

Finally, it has been suggested by anthropologists such as Geertz that all human beings have "aesthetic urges"[6]. Every society has some kind of art and entertainment for its members. The art in a society will have standards of form and substance, and these standards are related to the values, technology and social structure of that society. One of the interesting features of human life is the tremendous variety of aesthetic forms, but nowhere is there a society where the sense of the aesthetic is absent.

STAGE 2

We need now to pass from cultural universals to the application of cultural analysis to a particular society, using the seven universals outlined above as our general headings. As there is insufficient time and space for a detailed consideration of each of these seven parameters, I will then proceed immediately in each case to Stage 3 - that is, to see the cultural variables and the educational implications at the same time.

If we look at the education system of England in 1981 and compare it with the contemporary social trends, we will be able to identify a number of important failures to match the educational or curricular provision with the various kinds of social change.

But it is necessary to note at this stage that this is not necessarily a bad thing – if society is considered to be "moving in the wrong direction", it may be an advantage for education to resist or oppose those particular kinds of change. But in order to be able to make such a judgment, educationists need to be able to refer to universal principles of some kind – that is, the cultural variables have to be judged by criteria existing outside any one particular society.

Let us then look at the seven universals already identified (Stage 2) and then compare the English educational provision with that cultural analysis (Stage 3), bearing in mind such educational universals as the fact that education is necessarily concerned with "improvement", development, autonomy – all of which involve difficulties in definition, but have been extensively discussed elsewhere.

1. Social structure

A detailed cultural analysis of this particular item could involve a whole book, but the features of English social structure which would stand out as of particular significance for educational purposes would include:

(a) The UK is an urban society, with a very complex political, economic and social structure. But most young people leave school ignorant of that structure.

(b) It is an industrialised society. But education has failed to enable the young to live within that industrialised society: they have a very imperfect understanding of industrialisation; many of them are not educated in such a way as to gain employment, or to be able to cope with unemployment by being educated for leisure.

(c) It is a democratic society with a high rate of social mobility. But schools still tend to divide the young socially, academically and culturally rather than to encourage co-operation, social harmony and the development of a common culture.

2. Communication

English is the common language for the whole of the UK, but the fact that there are linguistic minorities in the UK is often ignored. Even for native speakers of English, the curriculum is hardly adequate. Oral language is comparatively neglected; most schools have yet to develop a policy of "language across the curriculum". This is partly a failure to get to grips with specialist forms of language or varieties of language such as the language of science, and partly a failure to relate everyday language to academic language of the classroom. It would also be necessary to stress that English is not the only form of communication. A scientific, industrialised society uses mathematics to communicate; in a democratic society much vital information is communicated by statistical charts, diagrams and symbols; increasingly it is suggested that we may all need to learn computer languages – there is a danger that as the microprocessor revolution progresses, society might be divided into those with access to increasingly complex information retrieval systems and those who have not mastered such techniques.

3. Rationality

The particular kind of rationality which is said to dominate our culture is "hypothetico-deductive reasoning".

But two points need to be made:

(a)   that children "learn" science without ever getting to grips with the underlying scientific methodology – even at A level;

(b)   they fail to distinguish between scientific rationality and other forms of rationality; for example, the rationality of poetry or music or art. Scientific rationality has dominated the curriculum without achieving an understanding of science.

4. Technology

In a highly industrialised society (or even in a society which is to be highly industrialised) technology is enormously complex. So much so, that no one individual can be expected to master the whole of technology, just as no one individual can know the meaning of all the words in a dictionary. Specialisation is inevitable, but schools have a function not simply to select for specialisation, but also to enable the young to have a general understanding of the whole of the culture including the whole of technology, despite this need for specialisation. The history of English schools of all kinds since the nineteenth century has been that lower status has been accorded to technology than to less "useful" forms of knowledge. This not only has the effect of making us poor competitors in the industrialised field, but also results in the so-called educated and less educated alike having an insufficient grasp of technological problems and issues in society. This was already the case before the advent of microtechnology and the computer revolution. The argument for all young people having access to mathematical, scientific and technological knowledge, is that of understanding important issues, rather than giving them access to jobs (that will be important for some but not for all).

5. The moral system

England is no longer a Christian society; values are increasingly secular. Our society is also multicultural and plural in other respects. Yet schools are required to persist with compulsory religious instruction and a compulsory daily act of worship (although it is not specified who or what should be worshipped). Most schools still have to make the attempt to teach elementary ethics, and to work out, on a basis of consensus, a moral code which they are prepared to transmit. The issue of education in a multicultural, multi-ethnic society is equally obvious.

6. Belief system

Although our belief system is categorised by value pluralism – i.e., we do not agree completely on all issues of value – it is still necessary for schools to have a policy on beliefs and values. One of the major concerns of sociologists since the time of Durkheim has been the danger of a society lacking a common system of values collapsing into anarchy and anomy. Durkheim saw schools as having a very important part to play in socialising the young in this respect. More recently, sociologists have concentrated on conflict and social change, and some have accused schools of promoting "false consciousness" in the young, by encouraging them to accept the false values of a capitalist society. But there are also dangers of a society which has no beliefs, no norms, no values.

7. Aesthetics

At a time of rapid social change, the standards, forms and media in the arts tend to change very rapidly. This also tends to produce a kind of cultural confusion. The general public and even critics and practitioners are themselves unsure of what standards or by what criteria aesthetic objects and process should be judged.

This makes for a problem in the education system, but schools have so far reacted very slowly to such difficulties. Schools offer a very limited range of aesthetic experiences: painting and drawing may be available, but what about sculpture, pottery or photography? Woodwork and metalwork may be available (for some, but rarely for all pupils), but as skills rather than exercises or design, or aesthetic appreciation.

There is also a tendency to focus on the aesthetic modes of the past rather than the developing modes of the present: for example, novels and plays will be more likely to be treated within the curriculum than films and television studies. There is also a tendency to divorce aesthetics from everyday life. One of the most common aesthetic experiences of many young people will be the interior design of their own homes; gardening, plausibly described as the most popular art form in England today, is almost totally neglected in schools. What I am suggesting should not be confused with low level and low status kinds of domestic science and rural science: I am suggesting that everyday activities could and should be related to aesthetic principles.

Conclusion

What I have suggested above simply indicates in a very "broad brush way" some of the problems which emerge from an incomplete cultural analysis. Much more detailed work is required within each of those seven parameters if we are to develop ways of planning the whole curriculum at the school level. Radical changes are needed rather than the time-honoured practice of looking at last year's timetable, tinkering with it to cope with staff changes, and calling that curriculum planning.

Notes

1   Dearden, R.F., 'Balance and coherence: some curricular principles in recent reports', Cambridge Journal of Education, vol. 11, no. 2, 1981.

2   Hirst, P.H. and Peters, R.S., The Logic of Education, Routledge and Kegan Paul, 1970; Hirst, P.H., Knowledge and the Curriculum, Routledge and Kegan Paul, 1974.

3 Benedict, R., Patterns of Culture, Routledge and Kegan Paul, 1935; Kluckhohn, C., 'Universal categories of culture' in Tax, S. (ed.), Anthropology Today: Selections, University of Chicago Press, 1962.

4 Levi-Strauss, C., The Savage Mind, Weidenfeld and Nicholson, 1966.

5 Chomsky, N., Language and Mind, Harcourt, Brace and Jovanovich, 1972.

6 Geertz, C., Interpretation of Cultures, Basic Books, 1973.

Chapter 2

RECENT WORK IN MORAL EDUCATION

Lawrence Kohlberg

The cognitive-developmental approach to moral education has its origins in Socrates' Athens. Socrates believed that there was a universal conception of justice which was rational, or cognitive. Whether rational or known through philosophic intuition, justice was to be loved, lived and died for, as Socrates demonstrated. Socrates believed that a universal conception of justice was latent in everyone (including Meno's slave), that it developed through levels, and that its development depended upon questioning, the arousal of doubt, and social dialogue. The research of my colleagues and myself has helped give the Socratic vision contemporary credibility. Our cross-cultural and longitudinal studies provide research evidence for the Socratic view of a universal conception of justice proceeding through developmental levels. The Stone Foundation project is one of the most recent confirmations of the Socratic hypothesis on the educational side.

It will be recalled that there were two features of the classrooms in which students demonstrated stage change. First, these classrooms had mixtures of students at different stages (no mixture of stages, no Socratic dialogue). Second, all the teachers in the "change" classrooms used good Socratic probes of reasoning; most of the "no-change" class teachers did not. (This was the only differentiating item on a 100-item teacher behaviour observation schedule). These findings not only reaffirmed our faith in the possibilities of moral discussions but our faith in Socratic dialogue.

The original test of the Socratic approach to moral education came by administering hemlock. Our research test of statistical significance is hardly as profound, but is easier to replicate by less committed educators. Philosophic commitment based on philosophic understanding is still required of moral educators, however. Moral education is still often considered revolutionary, as it was in Socrates' day. The only reason Socratic moral education today is less risky than in Socrates' Athens is because we can recall that our own society is grounded on a revolution oriented to moral principles. Our own society is grounded on documents (the Declaration of Independence and the Constitution) written from what we call a Stage 5 perspective, a moral and political philosophy of the social contract and of universal human rights. When Jefferson and others advocated public education, it was to prepare for citizenship in the new society, the constitutional democratic society. In our society, a person is a citizen when he or she can read the social contract, the Constitution, and sign it with informed consent. The true, American "right to read" is the right to read the Constitution.

While the American constitutional tradition provides some protection for a moral education for justice, we must still cope with Plato's conclusion from the execution of Socrates that education for justice must start with a just Republic ruled by a philosopher king. If the guardians of society were not just, who would educate children to be virtuous or just? American radicals pose the same question and question moral education without the revolution necessary for the Utopian just society.

The cognitive-developmental approach is compatible with John Dewey's progressive answer to Plato's despair about engaging in moral education in an imperfectly just society. In Democracy and Education Dewey wrote the second great treatise on moral education in a just society. Dewey, even more clearly than Socrates, claimed, "the aim of education is growth or development, both intellectual and moral." Dewey claimed that developmental (or Socratic) moral education could work in a society which was democratic, even though the masses or their guardians were not yet very just. Dewey, unlike Socrates or Plato, believed that communities (schools and societies) as well as individuals could develop, and that if education in a democracy could move the individual student to a higher level of justice, it would in time lead to the development of both more just schools and a more just society. Elsa Wasserman's article on the just community school is one statement of a revival of Dewey's vision. It recognises, like Dewey, that the moral development of a community of students is not the sum of the moral changes of each individual student. A school as a moral community can be either at a higher or lower level than the sum of the individuals in it. Our research suggests that in most schools the level of justice of the school as a social system is lower than the individual level of students, teachers, and administrators composing it. Wasserman's article suggests that a school based on concepts of justice and participatory democracy can be a community close to the level of its highest members and continuing to progress upward.

The movement of our approach to moral education from discussion of hypothetical dilemmas to a total concept of school as just community, deciding real moral-political issues, is still new and relatively untried, but it is rooted soundly in the philosophic and psychological tradition we have described, which can be traced from Plato through Dewey to Piaget and ourselves.

Moral education, unlike other areas of education, is a field in which one cannot achieve constructive results when one starts with confused or mistaken premises. If the teaching of reading had depended upon correct psychological and philosophic assumptions to get started, people would still not be reading. While research on reading has advanced since Athens, the practice of teaching reading has not improved much as a result. One can doubt whether the teaching of reading in America today is vastly better than it was in Socrates' Athens, in spite of our much sounder and more complex psychological understanding of the reading process.

With moral education, the case is different. While the statement in <u>Promoting Moral Growth</u>[1] of an approach to moral education may not represent a significant advance over isolated practices like Socrates' or Dewey's laboratory school, it is a vast advance over the practice of moral education as it now goes on in American schools, just as it is over the daily practice of the schools of Athens. This we say partly because research suggests little moral development through ordinary schooling (in our control groups), partly because of the philosophic and psychological confusions involved in the assumptions of most American moral education practices. Our comments about avoiding the arrogance of the psychologist's fallacy should not imply satisfaction with "commonsense" practices and thinking of teachers on this topic. I have commented elsewhere on the "commonsense" approach to education, that is, teaching a "bag of virtues" through preaching and reward. This approach was shown by Hartshorne and May to be not only ineffective but based on faulty psychological assumptions, although it comes most naturally to commonsense thinking about moral education. Another version of moral education practice currently popular with teachers is "values clarification". Values clarification is indeed a first approach to Socratic or developmental moral discussions but shrinks from hard dialogue and questioning of "why's" because it has rested on the assumption that values are relative to the individual. It rests on the faulty philosophic assumption of value-relativity, that everyone should have his or her own moral bag.

The most common system of moral education in America is neither "character education", "values clarification", nor a cognitive-developmental just community approach, but no conscious system at all, the "hidden curriculum". Its limitations can be vividly seen by viewing Wiseman's film High School or by reading my article on the moral atmosphere of the school[2].

We have said that cognitive-developmental moral education is not new; it has a 2,000 year history. Why is it a "bandwagon" now? The 1970's have seen flourishing, not only cognitive-developmental moral education, but also general scholarly concern by philosophers and psychologists in the United States, Great Britain and Canada. Why is there renewed interest in moral education, dead since the 1930's? The question receives an answer which is implicitly either conservative or liberal-progressive. Some would argue that this interest is a reaction to crime, Watergate, and the decline of traditional sexual morality, a conservative return to the social basics of moral order and discipline, like the return to traditional academic basics in curriculum. I propose instead that the current interest in moral education rises primarily from the rediscovery by liberals of the moral principles behind the liberal faith and the realization that these principles need to enter into education. Like the liberal reaction to Watergate, the liberal interest in moral education is a rediscovery in the seventies of the principles of justice behind the founding of our nation. The liberals in the sixties had lost awareness of the principles underlying liberalism, the principles of the Declaration and the Constitution. Instead of a faith in justice principles, the liberals of the sixties had faith in technology, in the social and physical sciences, and in rational political manipulation as tools of social progress.

As the liberal faith in rational instrumental social <u>means</u> has been disappointed, there has been a growing awareness of the need to have rational or moral social <u>ends</u> and principles of action and to embody these ends in education. This is fundamentally the meaning of the current interest in moral education. Behind this interest lies the principle of justice on which our society was founded. America was the first society whose government was grounded on a conception of principles of justice. The Declaration of Independence called these principles the self-evident truths that all men are created equal with inalienable rights to life, liberty and the pursuit of happiness. Watergate tells us that these principles have never been understood by the majority which every year votes down the Bill of Rights in the Gallup poll. The movement for moral education recognizes that in our society, all people must acquire, through education, some understanding of and acceptance of these justice principles. Watergate reminds us that justice principles cannot be maintained by force, laws, and government since the very leaders of that government failed to understand and support these principles. It reminds us of the need of an education for and through justice.

I've said that America was the first nation whose government was publicly founded on post-conventional principles of justice and the rights of human beings, rather than upon the authority central to conventional moral reasoning. This is Stage 5. At the time of our founding, our Stage 5, post-conventional or principled moral and political reasoning, was the possession of the minority, as it still is. Today, as in the time of our founding, the majority of our adults are at the conventional level, particularly the law-and-order fourth moral stage. The founders of our nation intuitively understood this without the benefit of research and designed a Constitutional government which would maintain principles of justice and the rights of all even though principled people were not in power. The machinery included checks and balances, the independent judiciary, freedom of the press. Most recently, this machinery found its use at Watergate.

The tragedy of Richard Nixon, as Harry Truman said long ago, was that he never understood the Constitution, a Stage 5 document. No public word of Nixon ever rose above Stage 4, the law-and-order stage. His last comments in the White House were of wonderment that the Republican Congress could turn on him after so many Stage 2 exchanges in favors in getting them elected. The level of reasoning in much of the White House transcripts was similar, including the discussion of laundering money. While the tragedy of Richard Nixon was that he never understood the Constitution, the triumph of America is that the Constitution understood Richard Nixon. It is not free citizens who are bound in "the chains of the Constitution" (Jefferson's phrase) but men who attain power without Stage 5 understanding or acceptance of the justice, rights, and principles enshrined in the Declaration.

The liberal reaction to Watergate has understood that Watergate is not some sign of moral decay of the nation, but rather, of the fact that understanding and action in support of justice principles is still the possession of a minority in our society, and that the moral progress of our nation has far to go. Watergate, then, reflects the slow movement of society from the conventional to the morally principled level.

The current sense of a need for moral education, then, is best conceived of as the demands which evolving standards of justice place on traditional conceptions of education and social-ization. The current concern for moral education represents an awareness of a demand for a higher or post-conventional level of moral principles in our national life. Citizens are no longer to be obedient soldiers or nationalist voters but voters or soldiers whose actions are to be governed by principles.

In terms of principles of justice, Watergate and My Lai both illustrate, not the decay or morality, but the failure of conventional morality to handle civil and human rights. This is not something new in national history. What is new is the situation in which the educational system is expected to develop a majority of citizens governed by principles once assumed to be the prerogative of a moral elite. Our educational system has failed to produce a majority of citizens who, like Lieutenant Calley and President Nixon, are only good at giving and taking orders.

What is specifically new to education is our expectation that high school students should be unprejudiced or non-racist. Implicitly, this is the expectation that students should go beyond the moral level of concern for upholding the norms of their group, family, and nation to the moral level of concern for universal principles of justice and respect for human dignity.

This expectation is, or should be, reflected in our current concern for desegregating the schools. Underlying the legal concern for desegregating the schools is the notion that our educational system should uphold the principle of respect for human dignity.

The Supreme Court's need to define a right to human dignity based on moral principles is involved in the enforced school busing controversy. The rationale provided by the Court for desegregation of schools has been "equal opportunity", the doctrine that schools cannot be separate but equal. This doctrine has rested on dubious statistical or social scientific evidence that educational facilities could not be separate and lead to equal educational achievement. Jencks' treatise is the last major summary indicating that school desegregation and compensatory education do little to promote equal opportunity.

If equal opportunity was a weak reason for school desegregation, it is an even weaker reason for enforced busing. Enforced busing is hardly leading to enhanced educational opportunity for either black or white students and it is clearly a restriction of liberty of white and sometimes of blacks. The only clear rationale for enforced busing is the equal right to human dignity. It seems right to enforce desegregation not because blacks will learn better but because a school is a public facility and denial of access to a public facility to blacks is a public insult to their equal worth, just as refusing access to a bus or swimming pool is.

We have pointed to a morally principled conception of justice in education in terms of busing. Such a justification for enforced busing depends upon a conception of education for justice and not just a conception of justice in education as equalizing educational opportunity.

The educational reform movement of the last twenty years has been a movement for curriculum reform, educational technology, and educational research and development. Beneath this movement has been a vague liberal belief in justice. Through educational technology, through upgrading the curriculum and methods of instruction, our poor and disadvantaged students would learn more academically and would have a fairer chance at life's goods and opportunities. Improved curriculum and instructional methods, it was hoped, could reach those students who would be condemned to poverty without academic skills. Together with curriculum improvement, school desegregation would raise educational opportunities and later life chances for the poor and black.

The seventies finds these liberal hopes for educational technology disappointed. The Coleman Report, the Jencks Report, and many other reports indicate that curriculum innovations and desegregation do not greatly change academic achievement and that enhancing academic achievement does not greatly enhance life chances for the poor.

The fallacy of educational technology and curriculum improvement as a cure for social injustice is suggested by Ed Zigler's comment when he took over Headstart. He said Headstart had been initiated with the goal of seeing the educational achievement of the entire country clustered at the fiftieth percentile. If society's resources are distributed on a competitive normal curve, improved educational technology may raise the mean of educational achievement, but it won't change the distribution. Educational technology will not help the students to deal with problems of social injustice unless the schools help students develop a more mature and stronger sense of justice so that as a participating citizenry, they can help to fashion a more just society. The seventies require a different approach to school reform than that of the curriculum reform of the sixties - the democratizing of the schools.

In summary, the current demand for moral education is a demand that our society become more of a just community. If our society is to become a more just community based on a democracy, it needs democratic schools. This was the demand and dream of Dewey which is still as unfulfilled as Plato's. I believe that the tortured movement of our society toward justice makes Dewey's dream both more possible and more urgent in the years ahead.

Dewey and the progressives argued for democratizing the schools and had little impact. Will the generation of school reform of the 1970's get farther? I believe it may. In some part this is because the theory and experience reported in Readings in Moral Education represents some intellectual advance over that available in Dewey's day, an advance which may yield a more effective educational "progress". In some part, it is because we have a more effective machinery for intellectual dissemination of "progress" to the schools than was available in Dewey's day. School superintendents and principals do doctoral research and theorizing on moral education in the universities, teachers take in-service workshops, and foundations give curriculum grants. More fundamentally, however, it is because just schools were a luxury for American society in Dewey's day, and today they are a necessity. American society did not need "education for justice" in Dewey's day. The same, I believe, is true for school democracy. While there is some return of the outward signs of renewed success for "education by and for authority" rather than education by and for democracy, this success does not touch either the rebelling of the inner city high schools, nor the inner alienation of the prosperous suburban schools. American education in the next decade cannot find its moral source in arbitrary authority or cultural consensus. Rather, it must find its moral source in the ideals of democracy and moral reason. I join the editor in hoping that these chapters will be of some use to those who are concerned about the education of young people.

Notes

Permission to reprint this chapter was kindly given by Professor Kohlberg and Winston Press, Inc. See, Scharf, P., Readings in Moral Education, Winston Press, Inc., 1978, pp. 1-15, especially 9 - 15.

1   Hersh, R.H., Paolitto, D.P. and Reimer, J., Promoting Moral Growth, Longman, 1979.

2   Scharf, P., op.cit. pp. 148-163.

Chapter 3

INTERNATIONAL PERSPECTIVES ON MORAL EDUCATION

Lionel O. Ward

In most countries of the world there is general agreement on the need to teach children a respect for truth, honesty, justice and patriotism, even if at times it appears to the observer that only lip-service is being paid to these laudable aims. These shared objectives reflect an international concern for the task of promoting moral growth or, more explicitly and directly, teaching moral values[1]. Despite this consensus there are wide differences of emphasis on the central objectives of moral education from one country to another[2]. In the U.S.A., for example, there is a strong emphasis on the virtues of freedom, truth and excellence, in the U.S.S.R. there is much more stress on the collective commitment, love of work and the promotion of internationalism. Indeed in the U.S.S.R. explicit teaching is such that in order to promote moral growth lists of moral components have been drawn up for use in formal training[3]. In France, some of the officially encouraged qualities are temperance, tolerance and kindness. Speaking at Sèvres in recent years, the Minister of Education, M. Haby, entrusted moral education to a 'slow, progressive impregnation', assuming that the values of civilization tacitly underlie school life, and that the models of man and of societies set forth in school extracts from literature would enter the subconscious of the pupils[4]. Similar arguments have been advanced for the role of history and literature in the British curriculum, and some of these arguments have the support of empirical evidence[5].

A fairly clear distinction can be drawn between those countries, such as the U.S.S.R. and Japan, whose educational systems are based on highly explicit ideologies and even constitutional foundations and those, like the U.S.A. and France, where there is a profound concern for individualism and fear of indoctrination. A clear illustration of the use of moral education to achieve national and democratic goals of justice and equality, stressing the developmental processes of moral education and the transmission of normative values, is Sweden[6]. Its neighbour, Finland, attempts the internalization of moral values on the basis of the values and principles stated in the Universal Declaration of Human Rights, a starting point for planning moral education in the Finnish comprehensive school[7]. Where a national policy exists for moral education there tends to be much more moral education actually being undertaken in schools than is customary, for example, in the U.S.A., Britain or France[8]. Sometimes individual states within a federation, for example Bavaria, have taken up the challenge, used their relative autonomy and introduced moral education into the curriculum. In the case of Bavaria there was little prior consultation with interested parties but, perhaps surprisingly, no controversy has been reported[9].

The fear that national policy-making, accompanied perhaps by inappropriate or misguided teaching strategies, might lead to indoctrination haunts the North American sub-continent. This fear is expressed in the Values Clarification Program of the U.S.A., an attempt to analyse the grounds for moral choice rather than establishing what those choices should be. In Canada, the Association for Values Education and Research (AVER) is an interdisciplinary group of researchers focussing on the competences, both conceptual and empirical, necessary for the morally-educated person. Teaching and learning units have been developed to expose students to value issues and some of the processes of normative reasoning. Teachers have been trained to use some of the processes of values education and courses have been established to expose students to a variety of philosophical, psychological and curricular approaches to values education[10]. However, as Benson and Engeman point out, there are risks involved in choosing either the purely instructional approach or the values clarification programme instead of using both critically and sensitively[11].

The empirical investigations which have been undertaken throughout the world, and notably in the U.S.A. and Britain, require little further publicising. They are based on the developmental schema of Piaget and Kohlberg, and have been concerned with situational moral reasoning, developmental sequencing and related problem-solving strategies[12]. The universality of the Piagetian and Kohlbergian stages has been investigated and largely confirmed in widely different countries, including Britain[13]. It is not surprising that a schema developed following investigations of American samples is applicable in Britain. Its applicability in Nigeria or Pakistan is perhaps rather more surprising. Significantly, however, in countries like these where there is a similar religious dominance but a different cultural background, moral reasoning is somewhat affected by the distinctive cultural values of the countries concerned[14].

It is possible that these increasingly complex empirical investigations have inhibited practical action in the schools and even been a substitute for it. In recent years it has been claimed by associates of Kohlberg that 'the major educational and curricular applications of Kohlberg's theory remain to be done' and that 'the theoretical understanding of moral development now available allows that practical work to go ahead with dispatch and promise'[15]. Certainly, as Kuhmerker has pointed out, concentration on the cognitive aspects has led to the neglect of the study of the role of empathy in moral development, which may in the long run be of greater significance in everyday moral decision-making. She has described the new stage-theory of M.L. Hoffman which comprises the development of person prominence, the capacity for role-taking and awareness of personal identity[16].

Americans have commented that the greater discussion of moral education in Britain than almost anywhere else has been helped by the decentralization of authority, the freedom of heads and teachers and the greater number of small schools[17]. Even in the less urbanized, industrialised parts of the world this concern for moral education is seen as a reaction to poor discipline inside and outside school, and the concern takes the form of education in personal relationships more than instruction in divine and metaphysical restraints[18]. This approach of the modern secular state is nowhere better illustrated than in India where, while there is some acceptance of the relationship between morality and spirituality and a recognition of the importance of the former, few states have provided for it. Oddly, this is due at least partly to the very diversity which is commented on favourably in the case of Britain, partly to the lack of uniform curricula and partly, of course, to the existence of more pressing social and educational problems. The result has been a reliance on what John Wilson has called the 'infection' model of morality. Moral education in India means obedience and conformity to particular values and practices. The distinctive Hindu values are non-injury, patience, personal purity and self-control[19].

What is revealed in different countries is something of the complexity of the relationship between moral education and social change. In many advanced countries moral education is seen as a means of taming some of the worst manifestations of social change, the reality of which is irrefutable, even if its impact on moral attitudes is unclear. Recently, Musgrave, replicating the work of the Eppels twenty years before, found that adolescents ascribed as much importance to individual choice as they had previously done, although the sexes were much more alike in their responses than they had been[20]. The impact of modernization, westernization and national security crises throughout the world has led, as in Korea, to the authorities providing schemes of moral education as a regular course in schools. The aim in Korea has been to reinforce the 'desirable' aspects of the Korean value system: self-control, sincerity, freedom, acceptance of responsibility, the development of traditional culture, committment to national development, a respect for humanity and contributions to world peace[21]. A more dynamic approach can be seen in Tanzania, where moral education has been instrumental in creating a society which exhibits African socialist virtues: citizenship, socialism and development[22].

Some societies, therefore, have clearly been more successful in achieving a consensus, or have suffered the imposition of a value system upon them. Both emphasise moral education as the work of the whole community. Where such success is achieved it has been independent of any specific constitutional or ideological foundations on which the educational system may be based. Christianity, one of the most obvious of foundations, is basic to the moral education of the politically and linguistically divided community of Quebec. While South Africa has been the subject of international criticism because of its apartheid policy, it is impossible to escape the impression that the official basis of moral education is Christian, however contentious some of the views of Christianity may be. But in South Africa the divided nature of the community influences outlooks, and for the black section of the community the fundamentals are tribal values and customs. Here, as in Pakistan, there is a strong emphasis on the family as reinforcing Christian ideals, and a strong family-school relationship[23]. Whether these mutually reinforcing influences of family and religion are always basic to the success of moral education is sometimes disputed. Not all countries are, like South Africa and Quebec, explicit in basing their moral education on religious teachings. While there are many Islamic countries, like Pakistan, for whom the separation of religion and morality is unthinkable, elsewhere, even where there are Islamic influences there are attempts to detach moral from religious education. It is more common, however, to see religion as such as only one of the forces at work in ensuring success in moral education. One writer argues that 'religion has only a medium range of effectiveness, whereas guidance and counselling and social, moral activities like current affairs and discussion are more efficient'[24]. One cannot help thinking that there is a confusion between religion as a school subject, whose limitations in influencing moral thought and conduct are acknowledged, and religion as practised by a community dedicated to the expression of religious values in everyday life. In Chile, attempts at moral education are complicated by the fact that the prevailing values are largely Catholic and essentially imported from Western Europe, though there is a broad acceptance of a philosophy which promotes the autonomous human being. In the unstable sub-continent of which Chile forms a part, however, there is an acute awareness that moral education can have significance only if it coincides with the will and principles of the whole of society[25].

In the U.S.S.R. not only is the school, as a formal organis-ation, designed to exhibit and sustain the moral values deemed important by the State, but the teacher is obliged even outside the classroom to hold informal conversations, and to reprove and show by example the moral aims to which pupils should aspire. Every opportunity for inculcating these moral values is seized; perhaps the most significant contribution is made by the youth organisations. In the Komsomol, the Pioneers and the Octobrists there is an initiation into values by collective activity, the selection of heroic models for emulation, the encouragement of thrifty activities and the unashamed teaching of patriotism. In the community at large a wide variety of pressures and sanctions tend to induce conformity to the norms of society[26]. The relative influences on moral education of home, school and community have been shown in countries like the U.S.S.R. to be equally important. But this is not always the case. Sometimes the schools can do even more than the society formally allows them to do. For example, the particular circumstances of Northern Ireland have shown the enormous influence of school, sometimes for good, sometimes for ill. It has been reported that children, when commenting on situations involving friendship, hostility and moral conflict revealed the school to be relatively important as a source of situations. In this case schools in Northern Ireland are seen as highlighting and reinforcing existing divisions but also as providing security and identity for children in an unstable, hostile world[27].

At the Fourth World Congress of the Comparative Education Congress, held in Japan in 1980, moral education was chosen as a major theme[28]. The instability of the modern world which makes evident the great need for moral education is also one of its most formidable obstacles; what is now required is a full practical application, on an international scale, of the considerable theoretical knowledge we now possess.

Notes

1 Hersh, R.H. , Paolitto, D.P. and Reimer, J., Promoting Moral Growth, Longman, 1979; Ward, L.O., Teaching Moral Values, Religious Education Press, 1969.

2 Bronfenbrenner, U., Two Worlds of Childhood: U.S.A. and U.S.S.R., Russell Sage Foundation, 1970; Weeren, D. J., 'Moral education in today's schools,' Journal of Moral Education, vol. 2, no. 1, 1972.

3 Bereday, G.L.F., Ruckman, W.W., and Read, G.H. (eds), The Changing Soviet School, Constable, 1960.

4 Fraser, W.R., Reforms and Restraints in Modern French Education, Routledge and Kegan Paul, 1971, p. 138.

5 Ward, L.O., 'History – humanity's teacher?' Journal of Moral Education, vol. 4, no. 2, 1975; Simon, A. and Ward, L.O., 'Age, sex, history grades and moral judgments in comprehensive school pupils', Educational Research, vol. 14, no. 3, 1972.

6 Kärrby, G., 'Moral Education in Sweden', Journal of Moral Education, vol. 8, no. 1, 1978.

7 Hakkarainen, P., 'On moral education in the Finnish comprehensive school curriculum', Journal of Moral Education, vol. 8, no. 1, 1978.

8 Weeren, D.J., op. cit.

9 Beattie, N., 'Moral education in the real world: a Bavarian case study', Journal of Moral Education, vol. 6, no. 3, 1977.

10 Kuhmerker, L., 'We don't call it moral education: American children learn about values', Journal of Moral Education, vol. 3, no. 1, 1973; I. Wright, 'Value/Moral Education in Canada: the work of AVER', Journal of Moral Education, vol. 6, no. 1, 1976.

11 Benson, G.C.S. and Engeman, T.S., 'Practical possibilities in American moral education', Journal of Moral Education, vol. 4, no. 1, 1974.

12 Piaget, J., The Moral Judgment of the Child, Routledge and Kegan Paul, 1932; Kohlberg, L., Essays in Moral Development, vol. 1, Harvard University Press, 1981.

13   Simon, A., and Ward, L.O., 'Variables influencing pupils' responses on the Kohlberg schema of moral development', Journal of Moral Education, vol. 2, no. 3, 1973;   Maqsud, M., 'Moral reasoning of Nigeria and Pakistani Muslim adolescents', Journal of Moral Education, vol. 7, no. 1, 1978.

14   Akinpelu, J.A., 'Avenues of moral education in some Nigerian secondary (grammar) schools', Journal of Moral Education, vol. 3, no. 3, 1974;   Haq. S., 'Moral education in Pakistan', Journal of Moral Education, vol. 9, no. 3, 1980.

15   Mosher, R.A., and Sullivan, P.R., 'A curriculum in moral education for adolescents', Journal of Moral Education, vol. 5, no. 2, 1976.

16   Kuhmerker, L., 'Learning to care – the development of empathy', Journal of Moral Education, vol. 5, no. 1, 1975.

17   Kuhmerker, L., 1973, op.cit.

18   Akinpelu, J.A., op.cit.

19   Seshadri, C., 'Moral Education in India', Journal of Moral Education, vol. 8, no. 1, 1978;   Yogeshanada, S., 'Moral education – a Hindu view', Journal of Moral Education, vol. 3, no. 2, 1974.

20   Musgrave, P.W., 'Some adolescent moral attitudes in three societies', Journal of Moral Education, vol. 9, no. 3, 1980.

21   Yi, G.Z., 'Moral education in Korea', Journal of Moral Education, vol. 8, no. 2, 1979.

22   McCormick, R., 'Political education as moral education in Tanzania', Journal of Moral Education, vol. 9, no. 3, 1980.

23   Potgeiter, P.C., 'Moral education in South Africa', Journal of Moral Education, vol. 9, no. 2, 1980;   Weeren, D.J., op.cit.

24   Haq. S., op.cit.

25   Vidal, G., 'Fundamentals of moral education in Chile', Journal of Moral Education, vol. 10, no. 1, 1980.

26   Ungoed-Thomas, J.R., 'Moral education in the Soviet Union', Journal of Moral Education, vol. 2, no. 1, 1970.

27   Ungoed-Thomas, J.R., 'Patterns of adolescent behaviour and relationships in Northern Ireland', Journal of Moral Education, vol. 2, no. 1, 1972.

28   Hiratsuka, M., 'Moral Education in Japan', Journal of Moral Education, vol. 10, no. 1, 1980.

Chapter 4

MORALS, RELIGION AND THE MAINTAINED SCHOOL

Paul H. Hirst

The 1944 Education Act legislated that in every maintained school there should be religious instruction and a daily act of collective worship. This legislation reflected not only general agreement about the value of religious education itself, but also the conviction of many that the moral standards of the nation could best be secured by these means. Many years later we are becoming deeply dissatisfied with the moral education our schools give, even amongst Christians there is a growing number who think moral education should be divorced from religious education, and compulsory religious instruction and worship seem to grow yearly less justifiable in a religiously open society.

In this chapter I want to look briefly at these issues primarily from a philosophical point of view, for they turn in part on two crucially important philosophical questions. First, is man's moral understanding necessarily dependent on his religious knowledge or beliefs? If the answer to that is yes, then any serious moral education must ultimately be religiously based. If the answer is no and moral knowledge is autonomous, then there is a prima facie case for direct specific moral education. Secondly, what is the status of religious propositions? Is there here a domain of knowledge or simply one of beliefs? And if the latter is the case, is it justifiable for state maintained schools to instruct pupils in one particular faith and to conduct worship in accordance with it? In arguing first for the autonomy of morals and moral education, I shall not be denying that moral principles and religious beliefs may be closely connected. Certainly they are in the Christian faith. Similarly in arguing against the provision in maintained schools of religious education, and worship, according to one particular set of beliefs, I shall not be denying the enormous importance of religious education itself. Nor is it my concern to argue either for or from a humanist or religious position in these matters. Rather I wish to look at them in the light of the philosophical character of moral judgements and religious propositions and I see no reason why both the arguments and conclusions of this discussion should not be acceptable to both, say, Christians and humanists alike. Throughout I shall be directly concerned with the Christian faith rather than with any other, but much of what I say is applicable more widely.

Of course no adequate educational conclusions can be reached purely on philosophical grounds but one must recognize the general bearings of philosophical considerations on these issues, however contentious or unpalatable they may seem. The intention here is to provoke further discussion, not to provide final answers.

I

What then of the thesis that moral questions are in fact inseparable from religious questions, that in the last analysis - if you really get down to the business - moral values rest on religious beliefs, for without this foundation there really are no reasons why one should be just, tell the truth, respect other people's property, and so on? In its strongest form this view maintains that for something to be right, is for it to be the command or will of God. 'Right' is 'doing the will or command of God' and thus our knowledge of what is right comes from our knowing what God wills or commands. Without this knowledge of God's will, men can only live according to their personal likes or dislikes for without this foundation moral principles just do not stand up.

Now it is one thing to maintain that whatever is right is also the will of God; it is quite another to maintain, as this thesis does, that for something to be right is just for it to be the will or command of God. On the first view, man may have a knowledge of right of a purely natural kind and in addition believe that what he thus knows to be right is also according to God's will. On the other view, being right and being the will of God are equated in meaning so that it can be consistently maintained that man only knows what is right because he can know what God wills. Moral terms like ought, right, good are here being so logically tied to religious terms that moral judgements have become essentially judgements of a religious kind, judgements as to the will of God. Because of the equation of meaning it is argued that man's moral knowledge rests entirely on what God reveals as His will in Scripture, the church or by His indwelling Spirit. This strong thesis really consists of two claims then. First that to say something is right, good and ought to be done, means that it is willed by God. Secondly that we only know what is right or good by coming to know what God wills.

It may, however, be said that few Christians go as far as to make the first claim on the equation of meaning, though more are prepared to accept the second claim as to the source and basis of moral knowledge. To hold simply to the second claim only and not to both is to subscribe to a somewhat weaker thesis. Nevertheless both positions firmly root moral knowledge in religious knowledge. The strong one ties a logical knot making moral knowledge necessarily dependent on religious knowledge. The weaker one, while allowing that other bases for moral knowledge are conceivable, denies that as a matter of fact we have any other. Both theses seem to have an appeal for religious believers but there are, I think, at least three different forms of argument why they must both be rejected by Christians, and among these reasons for rejection by others.

First, the second claim which is common to both strong and weak theses, that man only knows right from wrong by discovering God's will, is surely quite contrary to the empirical facts. Surely it is plain, unless one is so totally bemused by certain extreme forms of Biblical interpretation that one cannot see the evidence before one's very eyes, that men <u>do</u> know that lying, promiscuous sex-relations, colour bar and war are wrong quite independently of Christian revelation. The terms right and wrong, good and bad have meaning as ordinary everyday terms in human discourse. They are terms used for judgements for which men have perfectly good reasons which have nothing to do with religious beliefs. It is just false to say that there are no reasons for something being good or for my being good, other than that God has willed or revealed this. Certainly it is false to suggest, as have Christians who hold to an exclusive view of revelation must suggest, that outside the Judaeo-Christian tradition men have no genuine moral knowledge because they lack the revelation of God's will. How is it then that one can find the highest moral understanding in other traditions? Not in all, of course, but then all forms of knowledge are known in varying degrees within different traditions. In particular what of the moral understanding of Socrates and Aristotle based on the straight use of reason and observation? Can one honestly maintain that these people had no justifiable moral knowledge? I suggest that it is indisputable that they had a very great deal of it and that they did not derive it from Judaeo-Christian beliefs. Whether or not they lived up to this knowledge is another matter that I am not discussing, nor is it relevant to this argument that we now have moral knowledge than the Greeks had. What I am interested in is that they had moral knowledge and that it rested in fact not on religious revelation but on rational judgement.

Secondly, it seems to me that the second of the claims is clearly inconsistent with Biblical teaching on the basis of morals. Far from it being the case that the New Testament teaches that man's knowledge of right and wrong comes from revelation, the reverse is explicitly asserted. As Biblical doctrine is not my concern here let me refer to just one clear passage. In Romans 2.14 & 15 the Gentiles are categorically stated to have a knowledge of the moral law quite independently of the law of Moses. They have it by nature, we are told. Indeed the essence of the debate in this passage is that all men stand condemned before God because they know or can know the moral law and do not in fact live up to it.

Thirdly, both strong and weak theses are I think philosophically quite unsound. The strong thesis rests on the claim that what is meant by 'right' and 'good' is simply 'willed or commanded by God'. To say something is right or ought to be done is just to say that God wills it. Now this can be, of course, a way of winning one's case by definition - a prescriptive definition that legislates that we are only going to count as good or right what we assert is willed by God. But this surely is to be rejected as an attempt to make language do just what one wants when our ordinary understanding of the term just will not allow this. For if we inspect the meaning of right, ought, good, we do not at all find that their meaning is that of willed or commanded by God. There is, in fact, no necessary connection between the meanings of these two groups of concepts at all. If I say something is right, I am voicing a judgement on some action. If I say God wills this, then I am saying something quite different. I am describing a state of affairs. The terms have quite distinct uses in our discourse and do not at all mean the same. To draw a parallel I might just as well say that the term 'object' means 'what is created by God'. Of course objects may be created by God, but the meaning of the term 'object' is not at all the meaning of the phrase 'what is created by God'. Similarly what is good and right might, in fact, be willed or commanded by God – but to say that right means willed by God is just simply false.

From this emerges another point that a term like 'right', 'ought', or 'good' has a function which is logically quite different in kind from a phrase like 'what is commanded by God'. The first expresses the moral value of an action, expresses a decision, choice, judgement of value; the second states what is the case. There is a great gulf fixed between knowing any form of facts, knowing what is the case, and knowing what is right or good or what ought to be the case. To confuse the two is just to be guilty of a logical blunder. It is to be guilty of one form of what is known as the naturalistic fallacy, in which two expressions with fundamentally different uses are made to do the same job. It confuses statements or judgements of fact with statements or judgements of value.

But further, to equate good and right with what is commanded by God has disastrous results for Christian doctrine. For if what is good is by definition whatever God wills, then affirmations of the goodness of God, of His moral excellence, become trivial truisms – they are necessarily true by definition. In this way there is no significant content to saying that God's will is good, or even that He is righteous, for by definition things could not be otherwise. This is to make empty, truths that Christians hold to be part of a supreme and momentous revelation: that God is righteous, goodness and love rather than a morally indifferent or viciously evil creator. But if God is by definition these things, for Him to be otherwise is made just a formal contradiction in the meaning of terms.

Again, this equation destroys the Christian's moral life, for that becomes simply the obedience of will or command, no questions being asked about its moral nature. For to say that certain actions are commanded by God is by definition to say that they are good. The place of moral judgement in life is removed entirely; what remains is simply obedience, indeed supreme might becomes right.

But neither of these consequences is tolerable in Christian doctrine. That God is a supremely excellent being is not a definitional truism. Whether the creator is morally excellent or morally evil is a logically open question that must turn on evidence. Good is not just a label for the character of God's will or commands, no matter what their character may be. Nor is the Christian obeying principles that he does not know to be good. In that case good cannot be simply what God wills or commands. Man must have moral knowledge of good and bad, right and wrong, independently of any knowledge he has of God's will or of His Nature. It is in fact only if man has such independent moral knowledge that it is logically possible for him to grasp the significant truth that God is good and that His will and commands are righteous.

All the criticisms just made of the strong thesis are in fact also applicable, with only the slightest modification, to the weak thesis as well. To say that we will only count as genuine the moral knowledge we can acquire from knowing the will of God, is to win the argument prescriptively once more. To jump straight from what God commands to what it is good and right to do, is to commit the naturalistic fallacy all over again, even when there is no equation of meaning. Though not now true by definition, the doctrine of the goodness of God remains empty if the only basis of our knowledge of His will and the moral life is still reduced to mere obedience. From these criticisms it is surely clear that if Christian doctrine is not to run into serious logical difficulties, it must be maintained that man does have moral knowledge which he acquires by some means other than by divine revelation.

Why it has ever seemed important to Christians to think of morals and religion as tied together in these ways it is not easy to understand. For as was said earlier, to hold simply that what is right is indeed willed or commanded by God in no way commits us to saying that we can only learn what is right by knowing the expressed will of God.

An autonomous knowledge of morals is quite compatible with moral principles being also the will or commands of God. Take the parallel of scientific knowledge. A Christian might argue that the laws of the physical world are the laws commanded or willed for it by God. He might then unthinkingly subscribe to the thesis that because the laws are God's commands, the only way to know them is to be told them by God. Indeed he might hold the stronger thesis that for a scientific statement to be true is for it to be what God has commanded. As then 'true' means 'commanded by God' the only way to know the laws is to get at the very commands of God themselves. But not even the most fundamental fundamentalist holds that one knows the laws of the physical world by revelation. We know them by scientific investigation. The laws of the physical world may or may not be commanded by God; whether or not they are is quite independent of the fact that the way we know the laws is by scientific experiment and observation.

Similarly with morals. The thesis I have criticized maintains that because what is right is willed by God we must come to know what is right by revelation from God. But that moral principles are willed by God in fact tells us nothing about how man gets to know what is right or wrong. Just as man knows the laws of the physical world so man can also know what is right or wrong. Just as man knows the laws of the physical world so man can also know what is right and wrong, by the exercise of reason. Whether or not moral or physical laws are God's commands is another question. There is therefore nothing in my criticisms which is incompatible with maintaining that what is right is also willed by God. Nor is there anything incompatible with holding man's moral knowledge to be gained by the use of God-given abilities. Such general beliefs about moral knowledge are fully consistent with its being attained independently of specifically religious revelation in any form.

II

But if it is agreed that moral knowledge is autonomous, what is the positive relationship between morals and religion in Christian terms, for it would be preposterous to suggest there is none? Here it is only possible to outline briefly a philosophically more tenable position.

First, the prime significance of the Christian claim to revelation is surely that in it man has an understanding of the nature of God. In this, God is understood as a moral being who is righteous and yet love. From what I have said earlier this is, I think, only meaningful because we first know the meaning of moral terms and know ourselves to be moral beings.

Secondly, it seems to me a mistake to think of the Christian claim as being at all centrally one of having new moral principles. Surely the point is much more that there is in Christianity a crystallization of man's moral knowledge and the use of this as a basis for understanding the nature of God in moral terms and man's relationship to Him as a moral being.

This is in effect to say that morals are really more than mere morals. Wrong is not a matter of human relationships only, it is a matter of one's relationship to God. Wrong in fact is also sin. The Scriptures contain a great deal of moral teaching of course but surely the emphasis is not that these principles are only known because of divine revelation but rather that man's moral life matters in his relationship to God. I suggest then that to the Christian, man's actions can be known to be right or wrong on rational grounds, but he sees them as not only morally significant, for to him they have a religious bearing as well.

Thirdly, I see no reason to presume that any of the fully general moral principles in the Christian Scriptures are by their very nature unjustifiable on rational grounds. Maybe we cannot at the moment actually justify the Christian sex ethic - maybe we just do not know the facts on which to make such judgements. Maybe many Christians accept the Scriptures on this because on matters where they have independent rational moral justification they find the Scriptures trustworthy. There is nothing irrational about that. Still, we must be clear that such principles would have no justification if man had no basic moral knowledge on some other grounds.

Fourthly, the acceptance of Christian revelation does, however, add to the general moral principles that determine a person's life, certain rules that are specifically related to religious beliefs, e.g. that a Christian ought to worship God, give his time and money to Christian witness, etc. These principles are, of course, quite unjustifiable other than on Christian grounds. They are, however, thoroughly justifiable within such a context.

Fifthly, it is, I think, true that Christian teaching, in common with that of other religions, picks out among morally defensible ways of life a particular style of living, in that it sets up certain ideals and gives priority to certain virtues. The justification for these is I think specifically in terms of the religious doctrines. But at this level where I am thinking of the Christian concern to follow in some sense the pattern of the life of Christ and the virtues displayed with an emphasis of self-sacrifice and meekness, we have, I think, left the domain of general public moral considerations for something at a logically different level.

What thus far I have been concerned to show is that moral knowledge does not in general rest on any religious claims. If that is so, there is no reason why moral education must necessarily be given via religious education. It can, of course, be given as part of religious instruction but it follows from what I have said that unless that is done, fully admitting that man's moral knowledge must ultimately be found elsewhere in reason, then it is fundamentally misconceived and is a highly dangerous form of miseducation.

Of course a Christian will wish a child's moral education to be given its Christian setting. He will wish to complement what is achieved on a rational basis with instruction in specifically Christian moral principles to teach the religious significance of moral matters and to encourage a Christian style of life. What arises here is whether or not this Christian complement to moral education on a rational basis is the function of the maintained school in our society.

Here I want to argue that this is not an appropriate function for the maintained school but before I can reach that point I must say something about the place of religious education in general.

III

The fundamental philosophical question that arises for religious education in maintained schools is surely whether or not there is in religion a form of publicly accepted knowledge or belief that it is appropriate for these schools in our society to hand on.

In the forms of knowledge which are indisputably accepted in school there is no doubt whatever about the validity of the vast amount of what is taught. What is more there are accepted grounds and criteria in terms of which that validity can be defended. Further we teach as best we can, not only the truths and values, but their rational basis. In principle all these school subjects are treated openly so that no questions about the truths are ruled out. What knowledge we teach, we teach because it comes up to publicly accepted rational tests, convinced that all those prepared to investigate the matter to the appropriate extent will agree on the results.

Now religious believers make claims to truth and knowledge. If these claims can be substantiated, then religious knowledge ought not to be denied its place in school, and if worship is an essential part of such understanding, it too might rightly claim its place. But as a matter of fact not only do people differ radically in their religious beliefs, they differ radically about the basis of them, as to how we are to begin to distinguish between religious truth and religious error. Such radical difference on what the basis of religious claims is, may or may not be inevitable. Whether or not there is a domain of knowledge and in what sense, needs the most careful investigation. All one can do is look at the attempts there have been and are being made to substantiate these claims to see if they can in fact do the job. In so far as they can, religious knowledge surely must figure in our public education and the possibilities here will be looked at briefly later.

If in fact, as seems to be the case at present, there are no agreed public tests whereby true and false can be distinguished in religious claims, then we can hardly maintain that we have a domain of religious knowledge and truth. All that we can claim there is, is a domain of beliefs and the acceptance of any one set of these must be recognised as a matter of personal decision. If that is the case, as indeed many Christians would hold, what right has the state by legislation, and officially constituted bodies that draw up syllabuses, to lay down the beliefs in which children shall be educated? It is frequently assumed that such a decision by state machinery is perfectly in order provided the process is democratic. But what needs to be asked is whether the state should be involved in the making of any positive decisions in this matter at all. Where no issue of the general public good of the society is at stake, is there any ground for the state taking to itself the function of educating children in one religious faith? Is this not a matter in which the freedom of parents and purely voluntary bodies should be fully respected? Ought not the state to refrain most carefully from joining any particular religious cause and rather do all in its power to maintain the fullest freedom for religious education? I personally cannot see why we allow the decision as to which beliefs are to be taught to be taken by public bodies, for it would seem to me to be outside their legitimate province. And from this it would seem to follow that we ought not to permit state institutions to be involved in specific and restricted religious education. It is at least puzzling that the Christian church so readily accepts the principle that the state has a right to make decisions in this area. Would the church be prepared to accept so readily a democratic decision on this matter if it went against its interests? Would it readily accept the right of the state to decide that all children shall be instructed in Mormonism, Buddhism, or atheism? Would it not then wish to contest the very right of the state to make such a decision? If so, then the present position is one in which the church is guilty of opp-

ortunism and expediency, not one for which there is real justification. In matters where no public moral issues are at stake
the limit of any public concern would seem to me to be pre-
serving genuine religious freedom in every way and therefore in
education. This is not to say that in maintained schools there
ought not to be factual instruction about the beliefs that have
played and do play so large a part in our history, literature and
way of life. It is rather that positive instruction in the beliefs
and practices of any one religion should be strictly the function
of other agencies, the family, the churches and interested voluntary associations.

If, therefore, there is no public rational basis for religious
claims, then I see no immediate justification for maintained
schools having anything beyond instruction about these beliefs. In
this case it would seem appropriate for these schools to be
secular, genuinely uncommitted religiously. From this it does not
follow that there should not be independent religious schools too
for those who might desire them. What I am objecting to is a
national system of state maintained schools that is committed
to instruction, let alone worship, in any one particular form of
beliefs, even when democratically approved. There is, of course,
the possibility of having a range of maintained schools giving
different forms of religious education and training. It is difficult
to see how such a general policy could now be put into practice
in England and to many it would, in any case, be most undes-
irably socially divisive. It remains, however, a consistent possibility though the practical difficulties it would involve cannot be
gone into here[1].

To the position that is being advocated it is sometimes object-
ed that if we do not instruct children in religious beliefs we
implicitly declare that they are unimportant. Indeed there is felt
to be a danger that what are to many the most ultimately imp-

ortant questions in life might never be discussed in school. But adequate instruction about religious beliefs must surely include treatment of their significance for human life and in our society it is surely imperative that the part played by Christian beliefs in determining our way of life must be taught. This is not, however, to educate children as Christians. The intentions behind these two approaches are quite distinguishable and must not be confused. Further, it is mistaken to suggest that because a school does not instruct its pupils in one particular religion it necessarily suggests that these beliefs are unimportant. What it can quite clearly do is openly declare its recognition of the limits appropriate to its function as a publicly maintained institution. Such limitations are granted where party political beliefs are concerned and surely no one would accuse our educational system of being committed to a suggestion that these beliefs are unimportant.

Against the removal of religious worship, the prime objection seems to be that we should then fail to introduce children to a basic experience which they must have if they are to know what religion is about. But is worship a basic experience which beliefs make intelligible? Surely we must distinguish between on the one hand those natural experiences of the ultimate mystery of the existence of things and their contingency and on the other the experience of worship as an intentional act in church or school assembly. The former experiences may well be basic to any understanding of what religion is about. The latter, however, are experiences of a kind that are meaningful only on the basis of commitment to some specific religious beliefs. In this sense one can no more simply worship than one can simply think. One must necessarily worship something or somebody, just as one must necessarily think about something. If this is so, there is no experience of mere worship, but only the experience of worshipping some particular object or being. For if the activity is to be meaningful at all, it presupposes the acceptance of some beliefs, including the belief that there is point in praising and thanking and asking. But in that case it is quite impossible for a child, no matter how young, to worship unless he already accepts some religious beliefs, however vague. Seriously to take part in religious worship is therefore necessarily to be trained in an activity that is part of some quite specific religious way of life that assumes quite specific beliefs. I see no escape from recognizing that in so far as school worship is genuinely meaningful, it is this kind of training that it gives. If from what has been said earlier it is inappropriate for maintained schools to educate their pupils in one set of beliefs, it must follow that it is equally inappropriate for them to conduct worship in terms of those beliefs. This is not to say that the school should totally ignore the basic experiences earlier distinguished from worship. But it is to say that it should refrain from any activities, like worship, which pre-suppose commitment to some interpretation of these.

To argue in this way shows that if maintained schools are to be restricted in the range of knowledge and beliefs they instruct in, they must also be restricted in the range of training in the practical conduct of life that they undertake. For worship is not the only form of activity that is dependent for its significance and justification on particular religious beliefs. Earlier in this article attention was drawn to the fact that most religions – certainly Christianity – include some specifically religiously based moral principles. Equally they usually advocate certain particular styles or ways of life. If this is so, then the moral conduct of life in its more detailed positive aspects must depend on a person's beliefs. And if the school is not to teach any such set of beliefs it seems to me there are strict limits to the practical moral training it can give.

I suggest, therefore, that the most satisfactory position for the maintained school is for the religious education it gives to be confined to instruction about beliefs and for the moral education it gives to be confined both in instruction and training to the common pool of natural moral principles that all share. Beyond these limits we ought to recognize the freedom of the individual and of parents in matters of personal religious beliefs and those principles and practices of a way of life that especially depend on these. The only consistent alternative is, I think, the thorough-going pluralist system mentioned earlier in which maintained schools offering education according to different religious principles are readily available to all children.

IV

In all that has been argued so far about religious education it has been assumed that we can only speak of a domain of religious beliefs and not of a domain of publicly justifiable religious knowledge. At the moment no such domain of agreed knowledge exists and there are no agreed principles of justification. Maybe, by the nature of the case, such justification is impossible. That, however, has not been demonstrated as yet - indeed there are at least some signs of hope for the claim to knowledge in recent work in the philosophy of religion.

It is true that there is now almost universal agreement that the traditional 'proofs' of the existence of God must be rejected[2]. Few are likely to argue to-day that God's existence can be logically demonstrated in a formal argument from the meaning of the term 'God' or from the characteristics of the finite world. But a number of important attempts have been made at establishing the truth of religious claims in ways immune from the attacks on the 'proofs'. In much Protestant thought a basis for religious knowledge has been sought in personal spiritual insight, in intuition, in private self-justifying encounters with God, or in some commitment or decision[3]. If I have an experience of encounter how am I to know it is an experience of God and not an hallucination? If the core of the matter is simply commitment or decision, what is there in commitment that guarantees the truth of the beliefs? Private beliefs which lack rational justification may be true, but we cannot know that they are true without there being some public justification. And lacking that, we cannot lay claim to a domain of knowledge.

The height of sophistication along these lines is reached in the Barthian claim that God, being 'wholly other', is so beyond our concepts and reason that religious truths can only be known in a revelation which is under no obligation to justify itself to man. Religious reason is beyond reason and 'the very attempt to know God by thought is impiety'[4]. In spite of the plausibility of this language to many religious believers, to reject reason in this radical way is to make religious claims a mixture of the incomprehensible and the purely dogmatic. What is more, the thesis presupposes not only the existence of God but also certain quite specific beliefs about His nature and man's relationship to Him. Such assumptions at the outset of the pursuit and investigation of religious knowledge are quite unjustifiable. Indeed, the logically absurd call to reject reason in the name of reason is but an invitation to plunge into a morass of irrationality where again truth cannot possibly be distinguished from error.

In recent philosophy of religion there are, however, two attempts to deal with the meaning and justification of religious statements which seem to offer serious hope of much greater understanding of the nature of the claims. On the one hand a number of neo-Thomists have sought to re-express the traditional metaphysical account of St. Thomas in a way that can stand up to contemporary philosophical criticism. In this they have had considerable success. Maritain, Gilson, and others have argued that the proofs of God's existence are to be seen not as tight formal demonstrations but as expressions of a basic intuition or apprehension of the existence of things. This awareness is such that, once it is recognized what it is for finite things to exist, the necessary existence of their ground or source is recognized as well[5]. Mascall writes of the proofs as 'different methods of manifesting the radical dependence of finite being upon God'[6]. Farrer speaks of God being 'apprehended in the cosmological relation'[7]. Closely connected with these careful reinterpretations of the 'proofs' is a renewed emphasis on the analogical nature of all statements about God. Their meaning and validity are therefore to be approached according to the canons appropriate to this particular form of discourse, not those appropriate to the original natural context of the terms used. It is along these lines that Farrer, for instance, has attempted to establish once more a rational theology in which natural analogues afford a basic knowledge of God on which the claim to revealed knowledge can rest[8].

At the same time a number of philosophers less happy about the traditional categories have sought to characterize afresh the meaning and truth of religious propositions. To them religious statements are attempts to talk intelligibly about certain aspects of man's natural experience - his experience in everyday contexts, not simply that in such specifically religious contexts as, say, church worship. The view is that religious discourse picks out man's awareness that the universe is not self-explanatory, that human experience and knowledge are set in ultimate mystery and that this awareness breaks in on man in a great variety of circumstances. Some such experiences we have come to call numinous, others we regard as more mystical in character. Religious language is then regarded not as telling us facts about the inner nature of the mystery, but as attempts in parabolic or metaphysical language to relate and make intelligible these experiences. The only language we have is language whose meaning is closely tied to our experience of the finite world. When it comes to understanding this area of mystery and to answering limiting questions about our experience of it, then our language becomes figurative. Most developed religions, for instance, have come to speak of experiences of mystery as experiences of a 'person', but this is simply an analogy or picture by which to characterize the experiences.

When it comes to tests for the truth of religious statements, the point must be the adequacy of the pictures in making sense of the range and circumstances of the experiences. The tests must therefore necessarily be more on the lines of those appropriate for the 'truth' of literary works rather than those for, say, scientific theories. Professor Ninian Smart in particular has endeavoured to set out some of these tests in recent writings but the details cannot be gone into further here[9].

There are, of course, many points of agreement between neo-Thomists and this second group of philosophers and theologians. How far these can be made to extend is not at the moment clear. Along one or both of these lines, however, it does not seem at all impossible that an agreed rational basis for at least some religious claims might be found. In so far as a domain of religious knowledge can be established, the frontiers of the content of education appropriate to maintained schools must, it seems to me, be moved, so as to include it. The subject would then take its place alongside others in the schools. It would be taught necessarily as a mode of our understanding of human experience - the pupils' own and others - and the validated knowledge would be set in a context in which the principles and tests on which it rests would be taught as well. The nearest parallel in method of approach might well be that in the teaching of literature.

But perhaps this is just crystal-gazing. In the present state of affairs, whatever other considerations might imply,philosophical considerations would seem to suggest that the 1944 legislation on religious education is unjustifiable and that thoroughly open instruction about religious beliefs is all that we ought to have. Maybe, however, we live at a time when we can hope for much greater understanding of the nature of morals and religion and their relationship to each other. Certainly in the interests of enlightened educational practice we cannot afford to ignore the highly significant developments which at present are taking place in the study of these domains. For clearly, these developments could transform not only our ideas as to what education maintained schools ought to provide, but also our ideas on how best to set about those difficult tasks of moral and religious education that do properly fall within their purview.

Additional Note

The perspective on religious education which this paper expresses now seems to me unsatisfactory in two particular respects. First, certain paragraphs can be taken to imply that we have a domain of religious beliefs that may well be autonomous or logically unique in character but for which we have no unique truth criteria. This view I now consider untenable for reasons outlined in my paper 'The forms of knowledge re-visited'[10]. If meaningfulness necessitates truth criteria, then religious beliefs can only have that kind of meaning for which we have truth criteria, even if we cannot state what they are. At present, we are, I think, uncertain not only about the truth of religious claims, but about the kind of meaning they have. It is thus an open-endedness about the character of their meaning as much as about their truth that religious education needs to reflect. At its heart religious education is concerned with different claims to both meaning and truth. It is not concerned simply with meaningful but conflicting beliefs, amongst which we are unable to say objectively which are true.

This highlights the second unsatisfactory feature. To speak of teaching 'about' religion is open to many different interpretations. In one sense that phrase expresses very well what one wants, for it manifestly excludes all teaching aimed at pupils' coming to hold any particular religious beliefs. Understanding, not belief, is what is sought. But 'teaching about religion' is taken by some to mean a study of religion that is always one remove from actually getting to grips with the truth-claims religions make. To them it is a matter of studying the psychology, the sociology or history of religion. Whilst there is much that can be said for such studies, the elements of which will no doubt figure in any satisfactory school syllabus, pupils can only understand any religious position if they begin to grasp its concepts and therefore its truth criteria. Indeed any satisfactory study of the psychology or history of religion presupposes this understanding. But such understanding does not imply belief in or acceptance of, what is understood. My view then is that maintained schools should teach 'about' religion, provided that it is interpreted to include a direct study of religions, which means entering as fully as possible into an understanding of what they claim to be true. This will demand a great deal of imaginative involvement in expressions of religious life and even a form of engagement in these activities themselves. This must not, however, be confused with asking pupils to engage directly in any religious activities for the sake of these activities themselves. To my mind pupils should never be asked to worship, as this is to engage in an activity that presupposes specific commitment. The

58

maintained school should therefore never worship as a community.
How far in practice pupils should attend and take part in occasions of worship so as to come to understand what it means to
worship, is a difficult matter to which there might be no single
answer. What matters is surely that pupils fully recognise that
they are not being asked to do anything that either assumes, or
is intended to produce, the acceptance of any particular set of
beliefs. What pupils are asked to do is not simply to decide
on the occasions they shall or shall not attend, or what they
shall observably do on such occasions. It is as much a matter
of how they understand the situation and the point of what they
do. That point is always that they shall understand, never that
they shall or shall not personally accept the religious beliefs
under consideration.

Notes

1 See Beales, A.C.F., 'The Future of Voluntary Schools', in
A.V. Judges (ed.) Looking Forward in Education, Faber, 1955;
Cruickshank, M., Church and State in English Education,
Macmillan, 1963.

2 For a discussion of the ontological and cosmological arguments
see for instance Ninian Smart (ed.), Historical Selections in
the Philosophy of Religion, S.C.M., 1962; Philosophers and
Religious Truth, S.C.M., 1964, Chapter IV; Mascall, E.L.,
Existence and Analogy, Longmans, 1949, Chapters II and IV.

3 See Hepburn, R.W., Christianity and Paradox, Watts, 1958;
Ferre, F., Language, Logic and God, Eyre and Spottiswoode,
1962; MacIntyre, A.C., 'The Logical Status of Religious Belief',
in A.C. MacIntyre (ed.) Metaphysical Beliefs, S.C.M., 1957.

4 See Blanshard, B., 'Critical Reflections on Karl Barth', in
Hicks, J., (ed.), Faith and Philosophers, Macmillan, 1964,
especially pp. 162-180.

5   See Maritain, J., The Range of Reason, Bles, 1953, Chapter 7; Gilson, E., The Christian Philosophy of St. Thomas Aquinas, Gollancz, 1961, Part I.

6   See Mascall, E.L., Existence and Analogy, Longmans, 1949, p.71.

7   See Farrer, A.M., Finite and Infinite, Dacre Press, 1943, p. 45.

8   See Farrer, A.M., op. cit.

9   See Smart, N., Philosophers and Religious Truth, S.C.M., 1962; Reasons and Faiths, Routledge and Kegan Paul, 1958; Lewis, H.D., Our Experience of God, Allen and Unwin, 1959.

10 See 'The forms of knowledge re-visited' in Hirst, P.H., Knowledge and the Curriculum, Routledge and Kegan Paul, 1974.

Other issues raised in this chapter have been the subject of published comments and replies. See particularly:

Phillips, D.Z., 'Philosophy and religious education', British Journal of Educational Studies, vol. 18, no. 1, 1970.

Hirst, P.H., 'Philosophy and religious education: a reply to D.Z. Phillips', British Journal of Educational Studies, vol. 18, no. 2, 1970.

Shone, R., 'Religion: a form of knowledge?', Learning for Living, vol. 12, no. 4, 1973.

Hirst, P.H., 'Religion: a form of knowledge? A Reply', Learning for Living, vol. 12, no. 4, 1973.

Hirst, P.H., 'Education, catechesis and the church school', British Journal of Religious Education, vol. 3, no. 3, 1981.

Permission to reprint the article, 'Religion, Morals and the Maintained School', British Journal of Educational Studies, Vol. 14, no. 1 was kindly given by the Editor, and the above chapter is a further revision of that article.

Chapter 5

SOME SOCIAL INFLUENCES ON MORAL EDUCATION

P. W. Musgrave

I

A Sociological Analysis of Morality

Morality is probably most often described in terms of the sets of precepts that rule personal behaviour. Here a definition will be used which is both more general and somewhat narrower. As stated elsewhere, 'Morality will be seen as relating to the principles concerning how we choose to act in situations where there are consequences for others'[1]. This definition excludes many concerns for animals and some acts such as masturbation normally perceived as capable of moral interpretation, but it allows consideration of most actions defined socially as moral and above all it forces the analysis to be sociological by focussing upon the social nature of morality.

All human societies, be they as large as nations or as small as groups of close friends, are regulated, indeed we may even say defined, by sets of rules that sociologists have called norms. On this view societies are moral communities whose members are governed by norms. The members of any group will be concerned to preserve its identity and hence to guard the generally accepted norms. In this situation, someone will act as 'an agent of respectability'[2] with the power to sanction conformity or its lack by rewards and punishments. As Dahrendorf has put it, 'Society means that norms regulate human conduct; this regulation is guaranteed by the incentive or threat of sanctions; the possibility of improving sanctions is the core of all power'[3].

Yet there are often wide ranges of tolerance in interpreting any norms. Thus, in our society today husbands and wives may behave towards other women or men than their spouses in a wide range of ways. Choice is possible. Choosing how to relate to others is, therefore, at the very core of morality and, hence, in this analysis the teaching of how to make choices in social settings must be the starting point for moral education. Our choices govern our moral actions and since we have some freedom to choose, we have the chance to choose outside the range of tolerated behaviour, thereby either encouraging the use of sanctions, ultimately from those with power, to bring us into line or, where our deviance is not negatively sanctioned, causing the possibility of a widening of the behaviour allowed under the relevant norm. In the latter case a change in moral standards becomes possible.

The way in which we conceptualise choosing becomes, therefore, crucial for moral education. Usually in moral situations we take our principles for granted and act without much thought. Such decisions, following Schutz, can be called 'recipe decisions'. The 'moral man in the street ... has a knowledge of recipes indicating how to bring forth in typical situations results'[4]. However, from time to time crises occur and well-tried recipes fail to meet the social situation. In these cases where moral awareness has been aroused reflection is needed and principles have to be consulted before a decision is possible. Any analysis of moral choice, or indeed, any type of decision, must, therefore, examine the elements of such reflection. These may be seen to number four.

There is, first, a certain amount of sheer factual knowledge necessary for the making of any moral decision. At the interpersonal level a decision about whether to have sexual intercourse with one of the same or opposite sex will be most wisely made by those who know, for example, about methods of birth control and about the law. At the societal level when considering how to view a political party's policy on poverty overseas to which one will be committed by a vote in its favour one must know something of 'the third world'.

Next, reflective decisions demand knowledge not merely of facts, but of whom these decisions will affect. What beneficial or detrimental consequences will any particular sexual act have for others? Again, in taking part in these decisions at the soc- ietal level about policy towards poor nations we must know who will be affected overseas and at home. The question to be asked is: to whom is any moral decision relevant?

Thirdly, moral decisions, as is true of all social actions, dep- end greatly on how those involved interpret each other's beh- aviour. How do the partners in a sexual act perceive their action and what predictions can be made about the ways in which those to whom it is relevant and who come to know of it will perceive this act? A similar question can also be asked of decisions about moral decisions at societal level.

Finally, these three elements of any reflective moral decision have to be balanced. The difficulty of weighing known facts, possible relevances, and interpreted feelings of oneself and others against each other is awesome. It is, therefore, not surprising that in a small recent study out of five highly intelligent boys aged fourteen or fifteen in one school, four claimed that they often made difficult moral decisions not rationally, but by such random methods as 'toss-of-the-coin'[5].

Clearly, when one is weighing the information that one has available to make a reflective moral decision, one is guided by one's personal system of values. Gerth and Mills have written of a 'vocabulary of motives'[6], most of which is learnt uncon- sciously early in life. Examples would be the exhortations of parents to their children that lying and hurting others are wrong. A set of priorities will be brought to bear on the problem being faced. Thus, when a team captain has to tell a boy that he is not skilled enough to play in a school team, he must balance telling the bare truth against consideration for the feelings of others. How blunt he is will depend on how he orders priorities with the particular boy in question.

One well-accepted educational principle is to start teaching from where the pupils are. For those responsible for moral education this implies some knowledge of the vocabulary of moral motives of those whom they are trying to teach, particularly if they feel that they have some good justification for changing the moral views of their pupils. This is very often the position today where teenagers are involved. Something is now known about the moral views of teenagers. McPhail, for example, when starting the project for the Schools Council from which the Lifeline materials were developed, asked a large sample of teenagers how they viewed morality and moral education. They quite clearly gave top priority to consideration of the needs, interest and feelings of others. In addition, they felt they had the right and the freedom to challenge the 'traditionally respected adult sets of values and beliefs'[7]. Indeed, it is often because younger generations of teenagers meet this last view amongst their older peers that crises occur that drive them to reflective, rather than recipe, moral decisions.

In the context of moral vocabularies of motive, data gathered in another recent study of fourteen/fifteen year olds, made in England, Scotland and Australia, supports the following interpretation. The framework of moral motives has not changed much over the last two decades, though emphases within it have. Justice, personal responsibility, fairness, consideration for the individuality of others continue to be given priority. But within this framework of priorities girls have come to have views more like boys than was so; individuality has come to be given more importance and particularly it seems that those in the mid-teens condemn the labelling of their peers prior to a reasonably full knowledge of their attributes; in the matter of societal morality this group seems less utopian than those of the same age in the early 1960s. Finally, only one major difference between the three cultures studied was noted; the Australian teenagers were very much more critical of authority than their English and Scottish peers[8].

So far the argument has assumed that school is an appropriate place for moral education. There are at least two major problems about this assumption. Firstly, the question can be put: are teachers 'moral experts'? In view of their greater moral experience sufficient expertise might be granted them to teach morality as well as academic matters to their pupils, though in practice the division between academic and moral teaching will later in this chapter be seen to be a difficult one to make. There is a second difficulty. Although McPhail and others have found that pupils of secondary age want assistance from their schools in their moral development, yet some have also noted that teenagers may not see their teachers as those most fitted to help them in this field. For example, as early as 1962 Wright found that some teenagers in a school in a small town in Oxfordshire admired their teachers for the academic aspects of their personalities, but did not 'value them highly as persons'[9]. Twenty years later this position, especially in the case of teenagers in large cities, would seem to be even more true. Teenagers, therefore, will not readily view teachers as agents of moral respectability, a situation which makes moral education in many schools the more difficult to plan and teach.

II

The Institutional Context of Moral Education

In considering the views of pupils about moral education we have strayed into the next major stage of this analysis, the examination of the influence of the manner in which the school is formally organised upon moral education. As hinted earlier, the ways in which members of any organisation perceive its goals and workings will affect how it does and can operate. The desire of secondary pupils to be helped at school combined with their distrust of teachers as agents of moral respectability constrains the ways in which teachers can tackle the planning and the teaching of the curriculum in moral education.

Teachers themselves also bring attitudes to this task that limit the possibilities. Not a great deal is known specifically about these views. Teachers in English schools have traditionally accepted a responsibility for the moral development of their pupils as an important part of their role. In McPhail's study 80 per cent of the teachers 'mentioned ... the school's responsibility to help pupils develop an evaluative framework or to get on with others'[10]. Teachers in primary schools may well be in a very much stronger position to play this part of their role than those in secondary schools. Apart from any question of the much greater authority of the teacher over the pupils of a younger age range primary teachers almost always spend the whole day with one set of pupils and are, therefore, in a position to exercise a more constant and consistent moral influence upon their pupils than is felt by secondary pupils as they progress through a school day from one period to another under a number of teachers, each of whom has different moral views.

Parents are obviously very influential in the moral field, not only because of their early and constant moral influence upon their offspring, but in this context because of the support that they may or may not give the school in its efforts at moral teaching. Much evidence has shown that parents support the compulsory religious instruction given in British schools because they perceive it not as imparting a belief in some revealed religion, but as moral education[11]. Remarkably few parents, despite their own demonstrated agnosticism, withdraw their children from this instruction although the administrative mechanism exists for them to do so. The problem has become much more complex due to the changed religious composition of the populations of many countries due to recent mass migration. Thus, many Hindu, Sikh and Muslim children now attend British schools and there is as great a lack of agreement on the content of religious instruction as there is in contemporary standards of moral behaviour. One major difference between the two fields, however, on Australian evidence, would seem to be that many more parents define themselves as moral than as academic experts. They are very ready to criticise aspects of the moral, but not of the academic content of the curriculum[12].

Just because the role of the teacher in Britain has been defined in a way that gives it a crucial moral element, teachers have been seen as important agents of moral respectability. Durkheim, writing from French experience but with general applicability, called the teacher 'the interpreter of the great moral ideas of his time and his country'. Elsewhere he also wrote, 'A society in which education has become an important factor in social and moral life can no more abandon the educational system than it can the moral system itself to the absolutely arbitrary choice of individuals'[13]. On this very cogent argument all teachers are obviously likely to be held especially accountable for the moral lessons that they try to teach.

Since so much moral education, according to the logic of this chapter, must take the form of making pupils of any age aware of the choices being made or to be made and of preparing pupils to use rational processes when faced with making reflective moral decisions, teachers are continually likely to raise the possibility of changing currently accepted moral recipes or of challenging those learnt from parents. Such teaching may be seen to impart 'dangerous knowledge'[14] in that the young are being encouraged to behave near or beyond the limits of the range of tolerated moral behaviour. Unless such teaching is stopped moral standards may change and such change is nearly always seen as an alteration for the worse.

There is a paradox here in any society claiming to be democratic. The rhetoric encourages free choice, but, if teachers were to be really successful, much change would inevitably occur, since the powerful – be they employers, unionists, politicians, or those holding considerable bureaucratic power – do not in many respects behave towards those over whom they hold power in a way morally parallel to democratic ideals. It is for this reason that moral education is potentially a radical subject. Many teachers who question contemporary moral values, particularly in such sensitive areas as the sexual at the interpersonal level or the political at the societal level, are defined by parents or by those claiming to act for them, for example, educational administrators, as deviants. This process often leads to the disciplining of the teachers concerned. The way of the moral innovator, be he Socrates or some lesser figure, has been and always will be a hard one.

The environment in which any school works can have a big influence on how it is organised. A school that has a multicultural catchment area will have to take account of the differing moral norms of each culture represented. Schools cannot implement any form of organisation that their teachers wish, but have to bow to many policies that emanate from the local educational administration. Sometimes such policies can affect the moral education that teachers consciously and unconsciously give. Thus, if common secondary schools exist in an area the pupils can mix with a more representative sample of the population than in a selective system and the quality of interaction could put more emphasis upon tolerance between the different types of pupil. Another similar instance relates to coeducation. Pupils in single sex schools have been shown to learn different attitudes to the opposite sex from those in coeducational schools[15]. The same principle will be at work where mentally or physically handicapped pupils are integrated into normal schools rather than segregated in special schools. Where integration occurs more emphasis will also come to be put upon helping others.

However, even allowing for external influence on organisation, many details of structure are decided within a school. Thus, the way in which school assemblies or morning roll-call are run will have implicit lessons for how pupils come to treat those with authority. Many ceremonies that occur in schools either in conjunction with assemblies or apart, for example, speech or sports days, can build up favourable feelings amongst the participants which, if generalised, will influence views about loyalty. The manner in which school meals are taken will have implications for general ideas of civility and for learning the good manners that govern much of how we treat each other.

Many aspects of organisation are enshrined in the rules and regulations of a school. These may seem merely pragmatic. Yet such a common rule as that forbidding running in corridors is based in part in consideration for the safety and well-being of others. Not only does the quality, but the quantity of school rules carry moral lessons. A plethora of rules implies a distrust for free choice amongst pupils and will not only restrict the opportunities available to pupils to learn how to make moral decisions, but indicates both that initiative in behaviour towards others is not encouraged and that in general there is a narrow range of tolerance in moral and other behaviour.

Teaching styles also signal moral lessons. One recent English study found that 70 per cent of teachers feel that informal methods encourage responsibility and self-discipline, whilst opinions are almost equally divided about this in relation to formal methods[16]. More recently a large and much discussed study by Rutter and others in twelve secondary schools in London has shown that these beliefs are probably correct. In these schools a consistent pattern in the behaviour and academic achievement of the pupils matched the overall ethos generated by the teachers. This effect appeared to be not merely correlational; a causal relationship probably existed by which the ethos in large part brought about the outcomes reported. Two factors seemed important: the method of classroom organisation and the style of discipline used by the teacher. Where more praise was given, where punishment was less frequent, and where responsibility was given to the pupils their behaviour was better by the measures used in this study, and these included such moral behaviour as damaging property, writing graffiti, violence towards others and fighting[17].

School organisation may affect moral outcomes, but it is to the academic curriculum, or at least some parts of it, that most parents, teachers and, probably, pupils look for moral education. Religious instruction is the only school subject prescribed by statute in Britain. With this exception the content of the curriculum is at least in theory in the hands of teachers. Moral education is taught in some schools as a subject, but the important point to be made is that apart from these obvious places the moral development of pupils is consciously or unconsciously influenced in most academic subjects and extracurricular activities. Here there is only space to substantiate this position by quoting four academic examples: English, History, Social Studies and Science. In addition, the place of games will be briefly considered.

In teaching English, and the same principle would apply to the teaching of the native tongue in any society, for example, Gaelic or Welsh, a particular vocabulary of motives is encouraged. Pupils are taught to use and comprehend the metaphors of their language. For example they come to accept the phrase "the Nelson touch" and all that it implies. In addition, certain prose and verse is read and discussed which is approved by those choosing from all the literature available. In the chosen works many of the basic values of the society are celebrated. Thus, some pupils read Arthur Ransome's tales, set in the Lake District, because the children described demonstrate the plucky and adventurous personality desired by their school; others read Kipling's poem 'If', because of its approval of certain tough moral qualities. In other schools neither of these authors are read, since the qualities enshrined in their work are not seen as worthy of emphasis. Wherever literary criticism is taught in English pupils must disentangle the values demonstrated in the works read, but such an exercise must begin from some idea of what is good and what is bad. Judgements made on the texts being read will be guided by a specific set of values which it is hoped will be transmitted to the pupils. The teaching of English is very definitely a moral enterprise.

For as long as History has been taught in schools there has been a series of aims, moral in nature, in the minds of teachers[18]. The stories of national heroes, Nelson or Florence Nightingale, have been taught in the hope that they would be seen as moral exemplars. Great victories, for example that of Drake over the Spanish Armada, have been emphasised in the hope of building patriotism. Material has been chosen with such lessons in mind. Thus, when the Hundred Years War has been taught, the English victories of Agincourt, Crecy and Poitiers are remembered, but the eventual French victory is largely forgotten.

The various Social Studies provide many obvious examples of moral influence. Economics is taught from a basically capitalist position and little is made of the inevitable inequalities of capitalism so that such fundamental moral questions as how we treat the less well-off are begged. Similarly democracy is treated in syllabuses based on Political Science from the viewpoint of our version of democracy, so that the possibility of and methods used to achieve the greater participation at the local level found in what the Chinese call democracy are rarely mentioned.

Until recently scientists have tended to see their subjects as value-free when compared with particularly the Arts and the Social Sciences, but they have now realised that the questions they ask or fail to ask are determined by their values and, hence, they too are often involved in a moral enterprise. Thus, until recently their technicist approach overlooked problems of pollution and environmental or biological conservation. The recent birth and growth of Environmental Science as a subject in schools demonstrates the growth of an awareness amongst many scientists.

For almost a century games have played a central part in most British schools. They were always seen as important for inculcating moral lessons. However, since the 1960s a major change of focus has occurred. Team games had been seen as providing social lessons of, for example, co-operation, loyalty and subservience to a leader, as well as teaching individual qualities that have social consequences such as good physical health and knowing how to be a good loser. More recently the greater emphasis upon individualism in the social climate has meant that schools have given their pupils opportunities to play tennis, go canoeing or ride and to undertake such individual activities as the Duke of Edinburgh's Award. The emphasis in these extracurricular physical activities has changed and there has been little investigation of the reasons or the effects. Yet the aims are still essentially moral in character.

III

Implications for Schools

The line of argument presented here has at least three important curricular implications for schools. These concern (i) who teaches moral education, (ii) what is taught, and (iii) how a programme in this field is co-ordinated.

(i)   No teacher can avoid an element of moral education in his particular syllabus. This is as true of secondary as of primary teachers. Nor can a teacher escape moral outcomes from his teaching style. Yet his pupils may be wary of overt moral education. One possible answer to this difficulty has been to arrange that any formal moral education is given by non-teachers, for example, by counsellors or by outsiders of various types, such as visiting speakers. Counsellors are disadvantaged in some ways in that their role, often non-judgemental in nature, is sometimes unclear to both secondary pupils and their teachers[19]. The clear implication is that schools must avail themselves of all available sources of moral education, co-ordinating them so that each is used to the best advantage and to reinforce each other.

(ii)   A strong case has been made that choice is at the root of morality. This means that teachers must organise the curriculum in moral education around the act of choosing, making their pupils aware of the need for reflective choices from time to time and of the nature of the vocabulary of moral motives of themselves and of those around them, both their elders and their peers. The conceptual framework for making decisions becomes central to the development of any curriculum in moral education. That presented here has implications for the details of what will be taught. The problems chosen for study will need to be examined factually and in relation to the others for whom decisions will have consequences; an attempt must be made to interpret the feelings of all concerned; and, finally, pupils must consciously practise weighing all the material adduced as relevant to any one moral choice.

(iii) All academic subjects and many aspects of school organisation can have moral outcomes so that a policy covering the whole school curriculum is essential. Those teaching all subjects must be co-ordinated so that all the elements of morality deemed essential appear at some point and consistently throughout the curriculum. Now that the majority of secondary teachers are not upper-middle class, Oxbridge graduates and, of primary teachers, not upwardly aspiring products of a few colleges, and now that many teachers are not believers in Christianity, such planned co-ordination is essential where a century ago it was not needed. Furthermore, very inconsistent styles of teaching within the same school can cause doubt in the minds of pupils about what lesson is being conveyed concerning, for example, how those in authority should be treated. Therefore, there is even a case for attempting to co-ordinate some aspects of the pedagogy used in any one school. Finally, since the moral climate of a catchment area may change quite suddenly because of either national or local influences, constant evaluation of the total moral curriculum of any school is necessary.

Notes

1 Musgrave, P.W., The Moral Curriculum, Methuen, 1978, p. 22.

2 Ball, D.W., 'The problematics of respectability', in Douglas, J.D., Deviance and Respectability, Basic Books, 1972, pp. 326-71.

3 Dahrendorf, R., 'On the Origin of Inequality among Men', in Essays on the Theory of Society, Routledge & Kegan Paul, 1968, p. 173.

4 Schutz, A., Collected Papers: II, Nijhoff, 1971, p. 122.

5 Musgrave, P.W., op.cit. pp. 41-2.

6 Gerth, H., and Mills, C.W., Character and Social Structure, Routledge & Kegan Paul, 1954, pp. 112-29.

7 McPhail, P., Ungoed-Thomas, J.R., and Chapman, H., Moral Education in the Secondary School, Longmans, 1972, pp. 35 and 37.

8 Musgrave, P.W., 'Some Adolescent Moral Attitudes in Three Societies', Journal of Moral Education, vol. 9, no. 3, 1980.

9 McPhail, P., et al., op.cit. pp. 24-6; Wright, D.S., 'A comparativ study of the adolescent's concepts of his parents and teachers', Educational Review, vol. 14, no. 3, 1962.

10 McPhail, P., et al., op.cit., 24-6.

11 May, P.R. and Johnson, O.R., 'Parental attitudes to religious education in state schools', Durham Research Review, vol. 5, no. 18, 1967.

12 Fitzgerald, R.T., Musgrave, P.W. and Pettit, D.W., Participation in Schools? Australian Council for Educational Research, Hawthorn, Vic., 1976.

13 Durkheim, E., Education and Sociology, Free Press, Glencoe, 1956; Durkheim, E., The Evolution of Educational Thought, Routledge & Kegan Paul, 1977.

14 Johnston, K., 'Dangerous Knowledge: A Case Study in the Social Control of Knowledge', Australian and New Zealand Journal of Sociology, vol. 14, no. 2, 1978.

15 Dale, R.R., Mixed and Single Sex Schools, Vols. I–III, Routledge & Kegan Paul, 1969–74.

16 Bennett, N., Teaching Styles and Pupil Progress, Open Books, 1976.

17 Rutter, M., Maughan, B., Mortimore, P. and Ouston, J., Fifteen Thousand Hours, Open Books, 1979, pp. 182–99 and 206–10.

18 Ward, L.O., 'History–Humanity's Teacher?' Journal of Moral Education, vol. 4, no. 2, 1975.

19 Musgrave, P.W., 'The place of social work in schools', Journal of Community Studies, vol. 10, no. 1, 1975.

Chapter 6

THE DEVELOPMENT OF MORAL AUTONOMY

Derek Wright

It is necessary to begin with some brief reference to philosophy. The reason is simple. Before we can consider the development of moral autonomy we must have some idea of what autonomy means in this context. Sometimes the notion of moral autonomy is thought to imply the doctrine of moral relativism. This doctrine might be colloquially interpreted as 'everyone has to make up his own mind what his morality is, and no one person's morality is any better than anyone else's'. Such a doctrine is not entailed by the way moral autonomy is understood here, and indeed the doctrine would be rejected.

Notoriously, though we may live morality, most of us are far from clear about its nature. Part of the moral philosopher's task is to define it for us. Of course the essence of philosophy is argument; though the ultimate goal may be agreement, the philosopher's professional commitment is to ensure that no conceivable consideration or alternative viewpoint remains unexamined. Hence progress is slow; in regard to moral philosophy Warnock[1] has observed that 'there is still almost everything to be done'.

Nevertheless, the moral concepts the philosopher seeks to analyse and rationally interrelate are the embodiment of a moral life we all share in greater or lesser degree. To the outsider, and particularly the psychologist, it is evident that in his efforts to convince us the moral philosopher makes two kinds of appeal: he invites us to recognize the logical entailment of the steps of his argument, and he invites us to agree that certain key assumptions resonate intuitively with our experience of the moral life. He says, in effect, 'See how my conclusions follow from my premisses', and 'Don't my premisses ring true to your moral experience?'. The critic can therefore attack the conclusion in two ways:- by showing that they do not follow from the premisses and by either denying the intuitive validity of the premisses or drawing attention to other intuitively resonant premisses which are not consistent with the conclusions. One consequence is that philosophical 'positions' which are as yet rationally irreconcilable persist, in ever more subtle forms, because they are still felt to echo important features of the moral life.

An illustration might be the debate between subjectivist and objectivist interpretations of moral judgment[2]. For the moral psychologist, who is not qualified to enter the philosophical debates but who looks to the moral philosopher for some clarification of his area of concern, it is the persistence of these 'positions' or assumptions, in their constantly varying forms, rather than the existence of controversy between them, which affords clues about the nature of moral life. There are two such general assumptions which are relevant to our present concern. Both have been articulated and defended in a variety of ways, and though not universally accepted, yet command widespread agreement in one form or another.

The first is that the domain of moral discourse is itself sui generis and autonomous. The key terms in this discourse, words like good, bad, right, wrong, ought, ought not, have meanings outside the moral domain; but as moral concepts their meanings are distinctive and interrelated, and much recent moral philosophy has focussed upon analysing this distinctiveness and interrelatedness. The business of morality is not to describe how things are but how they ought to be, though to do this necessarily means taking account of how things are; and it is impossible to derive prescriptions about how things should be from descriptions of how things are. It is in this sense that morality is an autonomous, sui generis domain.

It is relevant here to look briefly at two ways in which this autonomy is manifested more specifically. The first is in relation to instrumental prescription (the classical statement is Kant's distinction between the categorical and hypothetical imperatives). Consider the following two arguments:- 'He ought to respect others; respecting others entails being truthful to them; therefore he ought to be truthful to other people', and 'He wants others to like him; only truthful people are liked by others; therefore he ought to be truthful'. The first conclusion embodies a moral prescription, and it does so because one of the premisses embodies one; the second, in so far as it is seen as deriving from the premisses, does not and cannot.

We can draw two general points from this simple illustration. Philosophers have attempted to articulate the differences between the moral and instrumental oughts. Among those canvassed are that the moral ought is universalizable, in the sense of applying to all people, and is overriding, in the sense that failure to act in accordance with it is only justified if some more pressing moral prescription supervenes. But for an individual to understand or perceive that there is a difference between the two oughts in the first place, he must already be a moral person; that is to say the distinction must resonate intuitively with his experience, for he could not be argued into accepting that there was a difference otherwise. The other point is that there is a kind of circularity in moral reasoning. The justification of moral prescriptions must always be partly in moral terms.

A second relevant way in which the autonomy of morality manifests itself is in relation to authority. The fact that God (or a parent or society) says that we ought to behave in a certain way does not entail the conclusion that we ought to behave in that way unless we insert another premiss, namely that we ought to do what God says we ought to do, and this premiss cannot be derived from anything God says. The fact that God commands certain actions does not, of itself, entail that those actions are right. This is not to deny that the religious believer will relate his morality to his religious beliefs, or that such beliefs may help to strengthen his commitment to act morally. The evidence for this is hard to find[3]. In fact, of course, concepts of God are manmade, and the moral consciousness of man has helped to shape them.

In short, morality is autonomous in the sense that it can neither be derived wholly from the facts of the world nor from authority, human or divine, since both are the subject of evaluation by it. No person can be argued into the moral domain from a position outside it; nor can he enter it through submission and obedience to authority. The individual has, so to speak, to discover himself already within the moral domain for moral argument and the utterances of moral authorities to carry persuasive force for him. The explanation of how he comes to be living within the moral domain is the province of moral psychology. The question Why be moral? is a valid one to ask, and its answer must be in nonmoral terms; but only a moral person can ask it, for it would only be a meaningful question for someone who was already moral. Whether or not a moral person can decide not to be moral is an open question; what seems sure is that it would be difficult to withdraw from the moral domain once in it[4].

This brings us to the second general conclusion to be drawn from moral philosophy, though it is really an extension of the first one. For an individual to merit moral approval it is not

sufficient that he does what he ought to do; he must also do it
because he ought to do it. If he acts in the way he does because he has been told to, or because he is afraid of punishment
or is seeking approval, or because he cannot help doing it, the
act, though it may conform with what morality prescribes, is yet
from the actor's point of view morally valueless. For an act to
be morally praiseworthy, the actor must have more or less freely
decided between possible alternative actions, and moral considerations must have been the decisive ones in the making of the
decision. This does not exclude the possibility that other,
non-moral considerations, perhaps of a self-regarding kind, are
coincident with and thereby reinforce the relevant moral considerations. In general though, we tend to reserve our stronger
approval for those occasions when moral considerations are in
conflict with, and override, other considerations; and our highest
approbation is usually limited to acts of supererogation, acts
which go beyond what moral considerations might reasonably
demand. A moral act, then, is one in which the actor acts out
of moral obligation, whatever other factors may be at work.
Now it is a characteristic of moral obligation that the individual
himself recognizes and assents to it. He cannot be coerced,
commanded or cajoled into such recognition. A distinction is
sometimes drawn between the morality of duty (obligation) and
the morality of the good (aspiration). However, the justification
for particular moral obligations must in the last analysis be
found in the creation or maintenance of states of affairs that
are judged to be good. Moral obligation cannot be in conflict
with such aspiration since it is logically dependent upon it and
may be psychologically generated by it.

One of the unresolved philosophical problems is whether the
concept of moral obligation necessarily entails an element of
motivation, disposition or behavioural tendency to act in acc-

ordance with it, or whether it refers only to a feature of the moral structure of situations[5]. But whether or not the concept entails motivation, it appears to be the case that when people recognize that they have a moral obligation they experience some kind of compelling force to act in accordance with it; at least most people do most of the time. The psychological problem is how best to conceive this compelling force of motivation. But it is philosophy that can help us to define what that problem is. On the one hand, moral obligation is laid upon us; it is cat-egorical, compelling, overriding, and has about it a quality of 'pure command'. On the other hand it is not at all the same as being commanded by some external authority or power. The individual autonomously recognizes that he has a moral obligation, and at the same time the obligation he recognizes exercises a constraining and compelling force on him, when neither the jud-gment nor the compelling force of the judgment are induced to him by anyone else.

To sum up the discussion so far. In referring to the morally autonomous person we mean two things that are intimately con-nected with each other. He does his own reasoning and makes his own judgments within the domain of moral concepts, the meaning of which he shares with other members of the comm-unity of moral persons; and his judgments are associated with a strong tendency to act in accordance with them, though of course this tendency may not on occasion be strong enough to ensure conformity of behaviour. People are more or less aut-onomous in relation to morality, but they cannot be moral people without being autonomous in some degree; and the degree of their autonomy can be taken as a measure of the extent to which they are moral people. The moral person is responsible for his moral judgments and actions, and such responsibility implies self-regulation and self-direction. This is not inconsistent with the fact that initially such a person may derive much of his moral belief from his social context; indeed, the existence of shared moral meaning presupposes it.

As a brief aside, something must be said about moral autonomy in relation to religious belief, since many people hold consciously to the conviction that their morality is founded in a divinely authorised rule-book associated with divine rewards and punishments. Our concern is not, for the moment, with such consciously held conviction, or the way people rationalise their moral beliefs (using that term without prejudice), but with the actual character of their moral lives, which may be quite different. If an individual's actual living is represented by some such formula as 'What God commands is right because he commands it, and I obey in order to win his approval and avoid his anger', then autonomy is minimal and it is an open question whether he can properly be called a moral person. Cultures which attempt to induce such a mode of living in their adherents are not propitious for moral development. Moral autonomy in relation to religion would be exhibited by a moral life which could be formulated as 'What God commands is right, not because he commands it but because I judge it to be so, indeed I would not believe in a God who did not command what I judge to be right, and I obey because it is right'. The developed moral person is one who understands, at least intuitively, that the domain of morality is autonomous.

So far we have focussed on moral autonomy as it is manifest in adult members of the community. We must now turn to the question of how children develop into such autonomy. There are two distinctive aspects to this process. The first is the development in the child of the capacity for moral reasoning and judgment, a development which culminates in an understanding of the autonomous nature of the moral domain. The second is the development of moral obligation as a motivation, disposition, or behavioural tendency to act in accordance with moral prescription. These can, and should, be regarded as two aspects of a single developmental process, though the relationship between them is not simple, and may involve a degree of dissociation.

It is the single achievement of Lawrence Kohlberg and his associates that they have laid a firm empirical and theoretical basis for our understanding of the development of moral reasoning and judgment[6,7]. There now exists reasonably substantial evidence that the way people justify their moral judgments develops through the sequence of stages that Kohlberg describes. No attempt will be made here to rehearse and evaluate these findings, nor the theoretical structure that Kohlberg brings to bear on them. There are, however, several points we should note.

Kohlberg has studied the kinds of argument that people use to justify their moral judgments to others. It is fully conscious and communicated thought. For our purposes, a stage may be defined as that set of salient considerations, or cognitive anchor-points, which functions for the individual as the more or less self-evident ground of the general defence he offers to others for moral judgments. Now it is not only possible, but it is plausible to argue that it is quite often the case, that the defence offered to others for a moral decision is quite different from the cognitive process, conscious and unconscious, of arriving at it. For instance, a child may ground his general defence of moral judgments in such salient considerations as the power and edicts of authority and the possibility of punishment (stage 1), yet display in his lived morality an independence of such factors, as for example when he keeps a promise, or protests an injustice, in the face of threats of punishment from authority. That is to say he can judge that he ought to act, and be impelled to act, in a way which is inconsistent with his general 'theory' of moral justification. If the analysis of the moral life given earlier has any validity, then Kohlberg's sequence of stages can be seen as exhibiting, among many other characteristics, a progressive convergence of the cognitive process of reaching a moral decision with the reasoning offered to justify it, until, at stage 5, the two are to a large extent isomorphic. It is significant that only relatively few people reach stage 5. It follows that for most people there is a greater or lesser discrepancy between their general theories of moral justification and the way they actually arrive at their moral decisions. The consequences of such discrepancy are unknown. We might hazard the guess that the more consciously elaborated, and more strongly believed, the theory of moral justification, the more likely it will be to influence the process of reaching a moral decision, and thereby be in conflict with, and possibly inhibit what the individual intuitively feels he ought to do. None of this means that Kohlberg's stages are somehow unimportant. Quite the contrary. They will form the basis of such things as advice given to others, the moral evaluation of other people, ideas about how institutions should be run, beliefs about punishment, and later will play a role in the formation of political and social beliefs. Above all, this analysis emphasises the importance of educating people's moral reasoning to the highest stage possible. One conclusion this line of thought would seem to lead to is that true moral integrity, defined as the unity and consistency of thought and action is only possible for those who have reached stage 5. We need not shirk this conclusion; for it would seem to be true if the developed understanding of the autonomy of moral reasoning is matched with an equal development of the autonomy of moral obligation. Without a strong sense of moral obligation and aspiration which keeps it serious and committed, moral reasoning can easily slide into rationalisation (in the pejorative sense) for not doing what ought to be done. We must therefore now turn to the question of how moral obligation develops.

Hitherto there have been three main ways in which psychologists have conceived moral obligation and aspiration. For Freud the super-ego is essentially founded upon self-hate and self-love, or, to put it technically, upon countercathected aggression consequent upon identification with the aggressor and upon libidinal cathexis on the ego-ideal brought about by anaclitic identification. Social learning theorists and sociologists have tended to subsume moral obligation and aspiration under the general processes of socialization, processes like positive and negative reinforcement and modelling. Kohlberg, as the main exponent of cognitive-developmental theory in this area, has changed his position somewhat over the years, but in a recent formulation he says 'the moral force in personality is cognitive'[8]. There seem to be two possible interpretations of this. The first is that 'moral force' is identified with the compulsion of rational deduction. Reasoning leads to the conclusion that a certain action is right, and the 'force' of the deduction becomes the 'force' to act in the prescribed way because the reasoning is about action. The second interpretation is one which abjures motivational concepts altogether, takes as given that the human system is alive and active, and sees the psychological question as why action is directed in one way rather than another through the cognitive steering mechanism.

The position taken here is that all these theories involve translating moral obligation and aspiration into something else, and that this is inconsistent with the philosophical analysis of the moral concepts themselves and with the experience of obligation and aspiration in the moral life. Instead it is claimed that there is a case for treating moral obligation and aspiration as itself, as a <u>sui generis</u>, irreducible feature of human functioning in the same sort of a way as we understand curiosity or bonding. The questions to ask are What are the conditions of its emergence? and What are the factors which shape its development? Psychologists have been loath to work with the concept of moral obligation and aspiration for some reason, yet it is difficult to see how they can do justice to the nature of the moral life unless they do. In fact only two major figures in this area, Durkheim[9] and Piaget[10], have more or less explicitly adopted it. The account that follows draws heavily upon their work.

It is sometimes said that Durkheim understood the moral life as submission to the norms and rules of society. This is unfair to him, for his position is much more subtle. He recognises, as does Piaget, that to be moral presupposes in the individual an attachment and commitment to society and a capacity for autonomous moral reasoning and judging. His central problem was to reconcile such autonomy with the fact that moral obligation is experienced by the individual, on occasion anyway, as 'pure command', as requiring from him things he may not want to do or may be afraid to do. He rejects the divine authority account of this, and finds the source of the 'pure command' in society. But by society he does not mean particular institutions within it, but society as a superordinate organism, or, in other words, society as a system of relationships between individuals which necessarily transcends those individuals. And it is not society as it is which is the authority behind morality but society as it ought to be. We could sum up his analysis of the moral life as follows:- the individual is attached or committed to his society and contributes freely and autonomously to the morality which defines how that society ought to be, but at the same time, because society transcends him, the morality to which he contributes is experienced as having authority over him.

The core idea behind this analysis is not made explicit by

Durkheim, nor is it made fully explicit by Piaget who carries Durkheim's analysis a stage further. We must therefore try to spell out what it is. Human relationships are systems, so that when an individual enters a relationship with others he participates as an element in a system of elements. A system can be defined as a set of elements organised in such a way that the system as a whole exhibits functions which are not present in the elements in isolation nor explicable wholly in terms of some additive accumulation of the functions of the elements. The system as a whole, therefore, exercises a constraining and modifying influence upon the functioning of the elements. We can then propose the formula that the 'pure command' aspect of the moral life, or the experience of moral obligation and aspiration, derives from the fact that the relationship systems to which the individual belongs constrain and shape his behaviour and are intuitively recognized as requiring his allegiance. For the individual his moral sense is intrinsically tied up with his sense of being related to others. It follows that the developmental roots of moral obligation and aspiration are to be found in the quality and strength of the child's first relationships, and that for those children who for whatever reason have minimal experience of such relationships will manifest a relatively weak sense of such obligation.

It was suggested earlier that we should regard the development of moral obligation and aspiration, of autonomous reasoning, and of the content of morality or the kinds of judgment made, as aspects of a single developmental process. We need therefore to show how each aspect can be conceived as a function of participation in relationships. Obviously relationships vary in a number of ways, and what we need is some preliminary, schematic classification which will enable us to infer that certain sorts of relationship are more propitious for moral development as a unitary process than are others. Since relationships are here conceived as systems, we can take our cue from general systems theory and begin by considering how relationships can be more or less hierarchical, more or less self-regulating and stable, and more or less open and closed.

The dimension of difference in hierarchical structure has been developed by Piaget in his concepts of unilateral and mutual respect relationships. To avoid confusion it is important to be clear that these concepts do not define relationships as such, but are ways of looking at, or drawing attention to, features in actual relationships. As Piaget acknowledged, real relationships are more or less characterised by both mutual and unilateral respect. For purposes of exposition we shall define these concepts of relationship in their extreme, purified and diagrammatic form. In unilateral respect relationships, one party has absolute value and exercises absolute power, control and direction over the other, and the other has no value, and submits and obeys. The dynamic maintaining such relationship is the exercise of power on the one hand and the fear of the consequences of disobedience on the other. The mutal respect relationship implies the equal value of each party, and each is respected as equal in the other's eyes. The activity which goes on between them is necessarily cooperative since neither has power over the other. The underlying and binding dynamic is mutual affection and sympathy.

Since in unilateral respect relationships one party is unconstrained and the other completely constrained by the dominant partner, there is a sense in which neither is constrained by the relationship as such. In mutual respect relationships, since neither has the power to constrain the other, both are constrained by the relationship between them. In other words, moral obligation is simply irrelevant to unilateral respect relationships on the one hand, and on the other, intrinsic to the maintenance and

development of mutual respect relationships. The optimal conditions for moral development are, as Piaget puts it, when the
child finds himself in the presence 'not of a system of commands
requiring ritualistic and external obedience, but a system of
social relations such that everyone does his best to obey the
same obligations, and does so out of mutual respect'[11].

In unilateral relationships, autonomy of reasoning is effectively
inhibited for there is no room in the relationship for it. In
mutual respect relationships the autonomy of each person is continually affirmed, for the relationship necessarily implies it;
each is answerable to the other in the cooperative process of
reaching agreement. Following an important distinction made by
Piaget, there are two ways in which we can look at the content
of morality. There are first the constituted rules, namely those
consciously held by the people concerned; and there are the
constitutive rules, which are implicit in the structure of the
relationship and shape the way the individuals live within it,
including the way in which constituted rules are reached. In
unilateral relationships the constituted rules are determined
wholly by the dominant member, whether or not he feels obliged
to assert the same rules for himself and the other. The constitutive rules essentially define the differential worth, status and
power of the persons so related. Such constitutive rules, which
discriminate among people in their fundamental worth, are alien
to our understanding of morality; but it is worth noting that
there have been approaches to morality which take as their starting point the innate racial or personal superiority of some people
over others. In mutual respect relationships, the consciously held,
constituted rules are reached by negotiation in which there is
equal participation by the people involved; the constitutive rules
which are implicit in the process of reaching such agreement are
precisely those which we would regard as central to morality,

such as truthfulness, promise keeping, equal rights, fairness and mutual caring. In mutual respect relationships, then, the relationship itself is the authority which generates the sense of obligation each experiences for the other, and the structure of that relationship embodies those principles and rules which we regard as the core content of morality. It does not follow that the participants in such relationships will understand this, except intuitively. But the continued experience of such relationships makes it possible for them subsequently to recognize the validity of such principles and rules when they are articulated.

Turning to actual relationships, it is evident that, for example, parent-child relationships will virtually never be wholly unilateral; mutual respect and sympathy are almost certain to be present in some degree. However to the extent to which they are unilateral they will not be favourable to the development of an autonomous sense of moral obligation in the child. Moreover, as Piaget suggests, unilateral relationships are inherently unstable, for the child grows up and is unwilling to acquiesce in his inferior status. It is important to note that Piaget does not equate parent-child relationships with unilateral respect, and peer relationships with mutual respect; both will have elements of each. But it is relationships predominantly characterized by mutual respect, whether with adults or peers, which constitute the most propitious setting for the development of intelligence, or self esteem and confidence, and of moral autonomy.

There are at least two other ways in which relationships may vary and which may influence moral development. The first will be called, for convenience, polarised versus symbiotic, a distinction which can be observed in mother-infant attachments and in marital relationships. By polarised we mean a relationship in which there is a high level of interaction between the members and therefore a relatively high degree of separateness in the perspective from which they interact; by symbiotic we mean a relationship in which the members keep close together but one in which very little happens between them. The former implies some degree of tension between individuals who have different points of view, the latter the relative absence of tension since the individuals tend to function like a single person. Clearly we would expect polarised relationships to be more effective in fostering moral autonomy. Then there is the distinction between closed and open relationships. By a closed relationship we mean one that is relatively closed off from those who are outside it. It is exclusive in the sense that the individuals in it have few and relatively tenuous relationships outside it, and the central relationship is relatively little influenced by these outside relationships. Mother-infant and adult 'in-love' relationships sometimes show this exclusiveness in marked degree. By an open relationship we mean one in which the individuals concerned have lasting and significant relationships with other people, and which is influenced by these other relationships. There is, as it were, a sharing of relationship across relationship boundaries, without, of course, the relationships themselves losing their integrity. A relationship which is too open in this sense would be likely to lose its character as a relationship. Experience of open relationships, we might suppose, would be likely to create in the child a generalised sense of relatedness to other people which in time is extended to strangers and even people who are never encountered, thus facilitating the extension of the sense of obligation from the relationship in which it first emerged. Both unilateral and mutual respect relationships can be seen as more or less polarised and more or less open, though this will not be spelt out here.

Throughout this paper no mention has been made of evidence. It would be possible to draw together from the literature on, for instance, mother-child attachment and delinquency, data which would be tangentially supportive of the scheme outlined. The goal here has been to outline an initially plausible theory to account for what is specifically moral in human experience. We can sum up the argument of this paper as follows:- The conditions least favourable to moral development in any sense are symbiotic, closed relationships of unilateral respect; the conditions which are most favourable to the development of moral autonomy in general and moral obligation in particular, and which lay the experiential basis for the later conscious realisation of the autonomy of morality, are polarised open relationships of mutual respect.

Notes

1 Warnock, G.J., Contemporary Moral Philosophy, Macmillan, 1967

2 Mackie, J.L., Ethics, Penguin Books, 1977.

3 Wright, D., The Psychology of Moral Behaviour, Penguin Books, 1971.

4 Williams, B., Morality, Cambridge University Press, 1972.

5 Frankena, W.K., Perspectives on Morality, University of Notre Dame Press, 1976.

6 Kohlberg, L., Essays on Moral Development, vol. 1, Harvard University Press, 1981.

7 Rest, J.R., Development in Judging Moral Issues, University of Minnesota Press, 1979.

8 Kohlberg, L., op.cit., p. 187.

9 Durkheim, E., Moral Education, Glencoe: Free Press, 1961.

10 Piaget, J., The Moral Judgement of the Child, Routledge and K Paul, 1932.

11 Piaget, J., op.cit., p. 134.

Chapter 7

THE MORALITY OF COMMUNICATION

Peter McPhail

Moral challenge is personal and immediate. It demands action. The most effective moral influences are those which best equip individuals to decide and act morally, to accept moral responsibility. Jesus said to the people, 'And why can you not judge for yourselves which is the right course?' (Luke 12:57). However, the trend within Western industrialised nations to move away from moral education based on external authority, religious or secular, toward a situational morality governed by individual decisions is historically recent. It has only become general since the Second World War. The question of the authority for, or justification of, such decisions always remains to challenge us. This chapter considers the possible nature and validity of this authority and how it may be developed to generate moral behaviour.

Traditional moral education in Western societies developed without systematic consideration. It was a function of home and school influence and church teaching. Compromise was expressed in the teaching and through the social conditioning of the growing child, the compromise between Christian doctrine, the demand of the State to accept that the end can justify the means, and the fears and hostilities of the people; their so-called 'natural inclination'. For example, Christ's plea that we make our enemies the objects of 'love in action' has never been internationally influential.

The relationship between ethics and popular moral education was tenuous in spite of, for example, the teaching of moral philosophy in the French lycée and the influence of Greece in the English Public School. It is probable, if one is to admit literary evidence, that the character and behaviour of individual teachers have been more influential in forming belief and moulding behaviour than the study of morals confined as it was in any case to a minority of children.

Hellenic influence expressed through Christian doctrine and reverence for the classics was elitist. Children were encouraged to refer to and respect external authority at every level from parent to ruler. Whether this influence was primarily Platonic or Aristotelian seems to have made little difference, though Plato's stress on rationality, ideas and concepts, favoured the intellectual rather than the aristocratic elite.

One might have expected that Kantian ethics with its emphasis on the universalisation principle and the morally unquestionable 'practical imperative', 'Always treat an individual as an end in himself and never as a means only', would have had more influence on popular moral education during the nineteenth and early twentieth centuries[1]. However, Nietzsche came to be preferred for nationalist reasons.

From the mid-nineteenth century up to the First World War, European belief in the rationality and fundamental goodness of man grew, rationality and goodness which could be expressed in system-building. Writing was evolutionary, was aimed in confidence at creating the good society through persuasion. The influence of Karl Marx, although he substituted 'matter' for Hegelian 'spirit' as the moving force for change, was to promise a society in which sectional vested interest would be abandoned for the common good. Christian theology was generally liberal, and many Christians believed in the possibility of establishing a kingdom of God on earth as the final expression and support of human morality sustained by the example of Christ's life and the internalised spirit of God.

European idealism did not die between 1914 and 1918 but belief in the inevitability of better things was never again possible. In particular, faith in the quality of leadership, democratic or traditional and hierarchical, did not recover, and with it went faith in the established forms of 'moral education'. Some countries looked for individual saviours from outside the establishment, became police states, and attempted to externalise the responsibility for the breakdown of pre-war civilisation. Their social education took the form of intense social-conditioning using the increased influence of the media, especially radio, to project, through newly developed progaganda techniques, unity of purpose and a single unquestioned version of events. Despite the official arguments which we offered, the appeal was to frustration and emotion rather than to reason.

In those countries which retained liberal democratic government, weariness, cynicism and the abandonment of traditional values encouraged totalitarian regimes abroad which offered a 'new order'. The romanticism of fighting for a 'just cause' had died on the Somme and at Verdun. A few volunteered to fight in Spain as the expression of political idealism but the mood favoured pacifism so that movements like the Peace Pledge Union in the United Kingdom gained in popular support. The world depression in the thirties further eroded traditional faith in God's influence on man and man's capacity to create a just and loving society. Many of those who had survived 'the war to end wars' found themselves at soup kitchens and in dole queues, apparently abandoned by the countries to which they had given so much.

In the democracies, traditional forms of moral education continued to 'go through the motions' though there was a deal of healthy criticism and unhealthy cynicism. One positive sign of a growth towards moral maturity was the influence of those who emphasised the inescapable individual moral responsibility for thought, choice and action. There was a renewed interest in existentialism with its emphasis on personal responsibility not only to choose, but also to act as best one can. Christian thought began to be focused on the 'How?' of moral expression and action. In the words of William Temple[2] 'There is only one ultimate and invariable duty and its formula is Thou shalt love thy neighbour as thyself. How to do this is another question, but this is the whole of moral duty'.

It would be an over-simplification to say that the Second World War, with its introduction of the atomic bomb and unprecedented cruelty off the battlefield, merely increased concern for the nature of individual moral responsibility and strengthened the call for a new, more sophisticated situational morality. In some ways war and post-war developments have reduced the potential for personal responsibility. Fatalism about the nature of change and the individual search for a means of escaping involvement in politics are increasing. Mass industrial society with its dependence on natural resources and the apparently inevitable dominance of technology, economics and collective decisions is, as Eric Erikson[3] amongst others has pointed out, a poor context for greater individual influence and the establishment of ego-identity during adolescence. Recent population pressures and improved transport have speeded up the development of multi-racial and multi-religious societies with their growing complexity, body of regulation and law, committee decisions and political autonomy. However, there is now no alternative to a radical approach to moral education based on individual responsibility and choice at the interpersonal level if we are to retain the word 'moral' in our vocabulary and not surrender to political social engineering. The question is, 'What form is moral education to take?'.

The post-Wittgenstein logical analytic movement in philosophy has encouraged interest in the 'language of morals' as well as developing the base and methodology for moral analysis and argument, and it is tempting to found a form of situational moral education on logical analysis alone. However, the movement has not generally contributed to the development of imagination, which Shelley described as 'the great instrument of moral good', and sometimes its claims have been misunderstood by those practically involved in the education of the young[4]. For example, it is possible and useful to distinguish in definition between 'education' and 'socialisation' whereas in human interaction we must recognise that there are always elements of socialisation in the attempt to educate. The philosopher who has done most to encourage a realistic empirical concern for the practice of moral education, while basing his work on logical analysis, is John Wilson, who offers a phenomenological description of morality made up of a number of components[5].

Wilson describes the 'morally educated' person as one who in his actions demonstrates the practical application of his component training and understanding. He leaves the insight into how this is to be achieved to the applied findings of psychological and sociological research into what I describe as the 'moral behaviour learning process'. The implication is that rational training and the understanding and application of learning process to curriculum, teaching techniques and, ideally, all human interaction, will make effective moral education possible; always supposing that individual choice is preserved so that the word 'moral' can be used legitimately.

The component analysis can be effectively used as a basis for a situational moral education syllabus provided that the situations used are the children's or young people's own and are real and relevant to their lives. It is neither necessary or desirable to abandon rules while retaining principles, as Joseph

Fletcher does, to make the morality situational and to guarantee individual responsibility[6].

The application of psychological learning 'know-how' about the motivation for moral behaviour extends what might otherwise be education for the intellectual elite into an approach for general use incorporating observation, sensitivity and imagination. We must recognise the practical and health importance of style and habit – of not attempting to make all human action which affects others the subject of conscious moral decision. Recognising the situations which demand conscious decision is a further legitimate concern for moral education. Life is difficult and demanding enough for the growing child without making every interpersonal situation a problem.

The tradition which Lawrence Kohlberg represents – that of research into, and the classification of, the development of the child's moral judgement – owes its origins and early evolution to Durkheim and Piaget amongst others.

Durkheim maintained that we are moral beings to the extent that we are social beings and identified three stages in the child's moral development: first, the behavioural response to discipline; second, what he calls 'attachment', meaning identification with the social group, so that the child's 'morality' mirrors devotion to that of the group; and third, autonomy, which is established when the young person understands the nature of social morality and applies it for himself. It is important to remember that Durkheim's use of the word 'autonomy' refers to understanding, internalisation and application. The source of judgement is still social. He regarded the acquisition of what he called moral 'attitudes' as necessary to higher moral development. These attitudes are responsibility, altruism, rationality and autonomy. His most valuable contribution was, in my opinion, to offer a description of the moral learning process in terms of behaviour as well as decision[7].

Piaget interviewed only 100 Swiss primary school children and based his account of the child's moral maturation on these interviews. His concern was with changing attitudes to moral rules. He believed that all morality consists of a system of rules and that the essence of morality is the respect which the individual acquires for these rules. This is a very limited view of morality, even for the period in which he wrote, and implies an equally limited approach to moral education which must be concerned with matters such as the child's sensitivity to the needs of others and practical capacity to put himself 'in other people's shoes', in real life situations as well as, finally, his ability to be morally creative, to make and implement decisions for change[8].

Although he was not consistent, the four principal stages of development which Piaget generally identified were:

1 The egocentric stage.
2 The authoritarian stage during which respect is acquired for authority figures and the restraints imposed by them.
3 The development in middle childhood of the notion of equality and justice - an 'it's fair, it's not fair' morality.
4 The acquisition of the concept of equity which implies the disposition and capacity to consider all the aspects of a situation - 'What was done?', 'Why was it done?', and 'Was it intended?'.

The fourth stage highlights obvious problems for a morality based on respect for rules, problems expressed by the quotation: 'Instead of looking for equality in identity, the child no longer thinks of the equal rights of individuals except in relation to the particular situation of each'.

Piaget's approach raised the question as to whether we can assume that it is possible to establish stages of moral development which apply to all children in every society at any time.

My work suggests that it is not possible.

Lawrence Kohlberg's[9] research led him to elaborate the child's moral development into six stages at three levels:

Level 1. **Preconventional**

Stage 1. No differentiation of moral values, the child is caught up in a punishment (and presumably reward) - obedience sequence.

Stage 2. Naive instrumental hedonism, during which the process is one of satisfying immediate needs. The value of human life during this stage is instrumental, is a means to the individual's contentment.

Level 2. **Conventional**

Stage 3. What Kohlberg has called "good boy - nice girl" morality. The value of human life is based on empathy and the affection of the family members towards its possessor.

Stage 4. Authority-maintained morality, in which life is sacred in the religious or moral order.

Level 3. **Autonomous**

Stage 5. The morality of individual rights, contract and democratically accepted law in which life is valued in relation to community welfare and universal human rights.

Stage 6. The morality of individual principles of conscience. Human life is sacred and universal human value is recognised.

Lawrence Kohlberg suggested (possibly not seriously) in Toronto in 1965 that there might also be a Stage 7 in which all life could be valued as is human life in Stage 6. This raises interesting implications for the extension of moral education in an increasingly ecologically conscious world. Perhaps we should concern ourselves more with the individual's moral response to his total environment? Is the immorality of man's morality that it is generally man-centred?

It is impossible to evaluate Kohlberg's research methods, findings and interpretation of the findings without an intimate personal acquaintance with his work. However the findings raise a number of questions, for example:

1. To what extent does the stage classification apply in different parts of the world?

2. How far is Kohlberg describing the child's rational potential with effective educational support?

3. To what degree do a child's stated reasons for a course of action describe his real reasons?

4. What is the relationship between professed arguments and reasons and the inclination to do whatever is suggested?

5. How far is Kohlberg's classification a rational construct and to what extent is it a psychological description of development?

6. Is Kohlberg right to suggest that individuals who develop through the levels and stages never revert to earlier forms of moral reasoning when many of us have experience of doing so under stress?

My impression is that the empirical validation of the findings could only be established in Locke's "cool moment". Certainly much of the American "values clarification" work based on Kohlberg's classification tends to generalise moral dilemmas, to use unreal situations and to ignore the importance of the child's real-life experience. In short, it ignores psychological motivation and behaviour learning process and offers an exclusively rational picture of moral behaviour learning based on discussion.

It is predictable that such an approach is attractive in a turbulent, highly emotional, multi-racial and multi-cultural democracy, sensitive and insecure about the possibility that B.F. Skinner could be right to identify "moral" learning as the outcome of operant conditioning. Most of us long for the triumph of reason, and it is not surprising that in all western societies which are having their traditional national characters rapidly changed and are faced with the unparalleled threat of obliteration, the tendency is to play down the more unpalatable facts about the way in which behaviour is learned.

In England, Hirst and Peters' work on the logical analysis of statements about education and Lawrence Stenhouse's emphasis on the neutral, impartial or "chairman of committee" role of the teacher are in each case adopted by some as exclusive approaches to moral education because of such anxiety. In countries with recent experience of the police state, the pressure to sterilise the process of moral learning by attempting to remove personal influence is even more marked.

However we do not favour reason by these evasions. For example, all communications, verbal and non-verbal, are value-laden and even the voluntary absence of communication expresses a value position. Reason requires that we recognise this.

I propose therefore in the remainder of this article to concentrate on the possibility of education for moral behaviour while supporting autonomy. St. Paul's complaint "The good which I want to do, I fail to do" only expresses one facet of the problem. The Irish priest who, after taking a moral education lesson in which none of his boys had scored less than eight out of ten for 'goodness' turned to me and said, "They wouldn't, you know!", was not even sure that they wanted to take the courses of action they had proposed. Our only hope lies in generating a climate for honesty, however challenging honest statements may be.

The Research, Findings and Programmes of the Schools Council's Moral Education Projects

It was against the background of the work already described that the first Moral Education Project of the Schools Council for England and Wales was established for 11- to 17-year-olds under my directorship in the University of Oxford in 1967[10]. The lack of systematic research made it imperative that we undertook our own moral behaviour learning research if we were to be of practical help to parents, teachers and children and to produce effective moral learning programmes.

I go into some detail about the approach and methods of the adolescent project, and the subsequent Schools Council project I directed in the University of Cambridge for 8- to 13-year-olds from 1972 to 1976, in the hope that it will be of help to those working on situational moral education in their own communities.

The first move was to undertake a preliminary investigation with 450 adolescent boys and girls in a variety of English schools into what they thought moral education might be and into what the schools should be doing in the interpersonal education area.

The principal findings were:

1. 70% of those interviewed said that school education should help them learn to live and work with others.

2. The majority thought that moral education was the process that develops when individuals and schools practise what they preach about the treatment of others and the environment.

3. When there was a conflict between what was said and what was done it was generally considered that what was done had the greater moral influence.

4. Moral education was therefore a facet of all education, of the total life of the school.

5. The maximum moral influence of the school was exercised when there was coincidence between teachers' rational and behavioural influence.

Other significant points which emerged were:

(a) There was a call for more personal education to meet personal need.

(b) There was insufficient education for change, education to help young people to be instrumental and operational in our rapidly changing society. A few, particularly alive to this need, stressed the importance in the moral sphere of what DeBono calls "lateral thinking", which calls on the total experience and imagination of the individual across academic subject boundaries to produce imaginative, creative solutions to problems.

The investigation indicated a number of adolescent difficulties connected with establishing identity and which gave rise to stress, ill-health and bad relations with the establishment. Many of the young people thought it nonsense to describe a society which was increasingly imposing law, regulation and prescribed ways of doing things as "permissive". Most were cynical about the value of more information per se and recognised honesty, humour and realism as supportive of moral influence. The "just" school was regarded as too cold to generate the climate for morality.

Those interviewed were generally honest about their situation when they thought the purpose of the investigation was to improve relations and was not to be used as a basis for moral evaluation or classification. Almost all showed signs of caring for someone and a few showed great sensitivity and imagination. At the same time they tended to resist traditional moral authority, conditioning through punishment and negative moral emphases. They were anxious about the moral standards, disharmony and destruction of political society, and were seeking answers to the questions "Who am I?", "Where do I go, and how?".

Above all it was clear that moral education would have to be focussed on the present experience and active day-to-day concerns of the young, and parents and teachers were to establish general motivation for moral action. This does not presuppose that traditional forms of motivation such as the power of example and rational persuasion are not psychologically effective for some adolescents.

The next stage was to identify more precisely the concerns and needs of adolescents and what happened when they were met or not met.

A modified version of the "Critical Incident Technique" was used by Flanagan and Crawford and Signori[11]. As its "decisive event" emphasis was reduced I named the method, "Significant Situation Technique".

I interviewed 800 individual adolescent boys and girls using tape-recording when acceptable and asking two questions:

1. "Give me one example if you can of a situation in which you think an adult treated you well."

2. "Give me one example if you can of a situation in which you think an adult treated you badly."

As a follow-up the subjects were asked questions to reveal how strongly they felt about the treatment, and what happened next.

A further 300 adolescents were asked the same questions about their peer relations, with the third question added:

3. "Tell me about a time when you found a situation difficult to respond to, or did not know what to do".

In this work we were conscious of the danger of confusing wants or mere expectations with needs and related, whenever possible, the outcome of welcome or unwelcome treatment to the well-being of the individual and his response to others.

The work yielded a rich crop of situations and responses which were summarised, recorded and classified.

Taking all the "good" situations together indicated that the adolescent description of "good" or "moral" was "taking others' needs, feelings and interests into consideration as well as one's own when acting", so that the implied description of moral education is, "any experience which disposes you to take others' needs, feelings and interests into consideration as well as your own when acting".

To those who are concerned about the naturalistic fallacy, the attempt to derive "ought" from "is", I offer this as the young people's operational description of "good", a description compatible with Kant's practical imperative and Wilson's prescription for the morally educated individual, as well as with the emphasis on **agape** in the Christian tradition.

Most young people interviewed accepted the obligation, at any rate in theory, to extend the good treatment they personally expected, to others, on the basis of common human sentiment. In this connection "ought" was used as the strongest possible expression of human obligation which transcended the more personal expression of opinion.

Looking in greater detail at what was "good" and "bad" in the situations and the implied obligation, a "Morality of Communication" emerges. This morality of communication is not only at the heart of what is good in the treatment of others but is also, from the stated responses to it, operational in effecting the contagion of moral behaviour and creating a climate for moral choice.

The morality of communication consists of:

1. **Reception ability**, meaning the ability to be and remain "switched on" to the right wavelength, to listen, to look, to receive the messages sent by others;

2. **Interpretation ability**, meaning the ability to interpret accurately the message which another person is sending, what he really means, what he really wants. This ability involves the capacity to read and interpret non-verbal as well as verbal cues, which is especially important as many verbal communications are for public approval and so disguise the basic feelings and needs of the individual making them;

3. **Response ability**, meaning availability and the capacity to decide on, and adopt, appropriate reactions to meet another's need when called upon to do so. It involves clarification, evaluation and decision-making, the use of reason as well as prac-

tical, psychological know-how;

4. **Message ability,** meaning the ability to translate appropriate reactions into clearly transmitted unambivalent messages.

The morality of communication is especially significant during adolescence because many communicational encounters are initiated by adolescents who depend on response to confirm them in a course of action, so that it becomes part of their adult repertoire, as well as to help them modify or abandon it and try something else.

The moral influence of communication is the result of the clarification and arguments it incorporates, and social conditioning, dependent on the practical concern expressed through the quality of communication itself, and the personality of the communicator. Even the most reasonable young people are influenced by adults' and peers' communicational skill and personality, however much we may advance the claims of pure reason.

The analysis of the encounters showed that social experiment, as described in the previous paragraph, reaches a peak during adolescence. Hence I refer to adolescence as, "The Age of Social Experiment", social experiment used by young people to establish themselves on terms of equality with adults, as adults.

Part of the art of moral education is to maximise the appeal of rational consideration in those new, or different, situations in which the individual cannot rely on "moral" habit or style, while making the young conscious of the influence of social conditioning.

My more recent work with adolescents in English speaking countries indicates that this description of adolescence in terms of "social experiment" remains valid. However, we cannot assume that the moral behaviour learning process will remain the same over a period of time or show the same pattern in all societies. There is a constant need for the kind of work I describe in all communities subject to rapid change if moral education is to be relevant and effective.

I have just completed (September 1981) for the Schools Council the preliminary analysis of 1500 responses of English and Welsh boys and girls concerning the good and bad treatment they have received and situations involving others in which they did not know what to do. In each case the subjects included a description of what happened next. They were also asked about what they most looked forward to, feared most, the good and bad things about living in 1981 and what, if anything, they would like to see done about them.

The findings confirm the central role of treatment and style of inter-personal communication in forming the individual's attitude towards, and response to, others during childhood and youth, but there have been significant changes in response since the late 1960's and early '70's. There appears to be less autonomous decision and social experiment amongst adolescents and there are signs of greater dependence and fatalism especially in the 14 – 16+ age groups. The contemporary acute concerns, which increase as boys and girls grow older, are with economic conditions, especially unemployment, moral decline particularly as reflected by aggression, violence and nuclear policy, and the inadequacy of political leadership.

It is of especial significance that the media have become more influential in moulding attitudes and behaviour and that much of that influence is destructive. Our schools clearly ought to devote more time to the development of judgement about contemporary issues and to helping individuals become as morally independent as possible. However, it seems unlikely that a morality of communication in school will effectively change attidues and behaviour for the better if those concerned about moral education do not recognise and respond to the priority of creating the national and international caring society. In brief, we cannot justify the gulf between public and private morality over matters such as the use of force.

For the pre-adolescent project[12], we also used "Significant Situation Technique", but as a result of preliminary work on the use of the words "good" and "bad" we asked the following questions:

1. Write and draw about a time when somebody made you feel pleased, or happy.

2. Write and draw about a time when somebody made you feel frightened, angry or unhappy.

3. Write and draw about a time when you were with somebody else (or other people) and you were not sure what to do.

In each case the children were asked the further question "What did you do?".

We worked across the ability range, and when children could not express themselves adequately in writing, tape interviews were used.

Drawing was introduced on the suggestion of a colleague, David Middleton who, rightly as it turned out, maintained that significant detail and greater affective depth would be made available to us as a result.

This time, almost 4000 children in a variety of English and Welsh schools took part, and we were dependent on the good will of the local education authorities and teachers, who administered the questions for us. Each child anonymously posted his or her responses to the project in sealed envelopes, an arrangement intended by the project organisers to encourage honesty and reduce anxiety.

It had been our intention to involve parents in the research – and clearly this should be done in future work – but time, and more particularly administrative anxiety, prevented this.

The children's situations were recorded, summarised, classified and made the subject of a computer programme. In the research report the situations quoted retain the original form of expression[13]. In the materials developed for school use the original expression is preserved as far as is consistent with teachers' demands for correct spelling, sound grammar and punctuation.

The central influence of the morality of communication and the contagion of behaviour were again established, but the pre-adolescent moral behaviour learning process differed significantly from the adolescent process. Basic motivation for considerate behaviour, especially for the younger children, depended on affiliation with significant adults. Parents were the most important points of reference, followed by close relations, adult friends of the family, and teachers. More of the situations quoted were home - or neighbourhood - based than in the adolescent survey. Apart from adults, contacts with peers, animals, places and things were influential in that order.

The eight- to eleven-year-olds were most happy, secure and effective when there was a consistent structure of rules for behaviour administered in affection. This was the base from which their practical concern for others grew. At the same time there was an increasing need for experimental and creative moral learning, often expressed in play independent of adults. As Niko Tinbergen has pointed out, play is of primary importance to the education of the human young, which often lacks biological balance because of its concentration on work in the classroom[14].

I therefore see the period of 8 to 13 as "the age of dependence and play" during which the individual moves from a secure base to increasing independence in choice and behaviour. The ideal balance between structure and freedom for a specific child is a matter of judgement for concerned adults, judgement which depends on the communication of the child and the interpretation ability of the adult.

Adult social conditioning has most influence in early childhood, so that is the period when we have greatest responsibility for what we encourage and inhibit.

During adolescence the most common cause of breakdown in adult-adolescent relations is over-zealous pressure to conform, not to basic morality, but to the norms and practices of the previous generation. In pre-adolescence, breakdown is more often associated with adult failure to supply ground-rules, predictability and fundamental security.

It is essential, not only that we realise that moral education of some kind is a facet of all experiences, unplanned as well as planned, but that we make it clear to children and young people that we recognise this. This is especially important when the growing child begins to identify and comment on the low standards of public (political) morality, compared with what is expected and usually achieved between friends. However, a planned and continuously refined school curriculum to develop moral sensitivity, choice and action is valuable.

Ideally, any moral education curriculum should be assessed and developed on a large scale before it is introduced. One of the great advantages of specially funded projects is that they can have the time and support to do this; for example, our pre-adolescent materials were tried out in over 80 schools before they were revised for publication.

The way in which we evaluate moral education material and technique is important if we are to set the tone for continuing work. Material is used in a multi-factorial situation, but this does not mean that we must depend on guesswork in evaluating it. The observer's comments, be he project member or teacher, can be based on clearly described objectives, and his skill when he establishes a morality of communication with children or young people steadily increases. In particular we should not be afraid of taking into account professional comments on the changing ethos and personal relations in a school. When a number of individuals contribute their comments, the extravagantly optimistic or pessimistic impressions become easier to identify. The students' enjoyment of and enthusiasm for the work are vitally important because they demonstrate relevance and positive motivation.

I believe it is best not to attempt to evaluate materials in laboratory conditions, even if they can be established, because the control of factors itself is unreal and encourages unreal findings. Verbal testing and examination puts the emphasis on words and not behaviour and introduced the wrong, competitive atmosphere. Above all, moral education material should never be used in punishment situations.

Teaching techniques using children's and adolescent's real-life situations should include:

1. A choice of situations whenever possible;
2. The use of humour and "light touch";
3. Simulation and role-play as well as discussion;
4. The use of the third person as long as the boys and girls wish;
5. A wide range of activities including, for example, art work as well as writing;
6. The movement towards real-life involvement with others, and work for others.

In this last connection what Alec Dickson, the founder of Voluntary Service Overseas and director of Community Service Volunteers, has to say is highly significant. Our aim should always be to sustain the interest, active involvement and sense of achievement which depend on relevance, challenge and the richness of our experience. We move from what individuals actually do in situations through experiencing, doing and discussing to the point when what I "ought" to do ceases to be an abstraction and becomes a way of life[15].

Materials should follow a psychological and logical progression based on what we know of learning. In the Lifeline programme, which we prepared for adolescents, the movement is from sensitivity - and consequences, work in simple dyadic situations, through the added complexity of small groups and the conflicts between groups, to the big, world problems in which the emphasis is still on relevant experience and the concerns demonstrated in the research data[16].

In Startline, the pre-adolescent programme, the progression is from sensitivity - with special emphasis on the use of photographs of those of different ages and from different classes and races - through what the child experiences and does, to the introduction of choice, always in situations familiar and of interest to the children[17].

In the case of both Lifeline and Startline the development of the work should lead to "spin-off" work based on the concerns and experiences of young people, parents and teachers living together here and now. An important point to remember is that no sequence of materials is sacrosanct. It is always necessary to move back to earlier kinds of work when a group detects the need, **"reculer"** pour mieux sauter". Furthermore, there are no once-and-for-all programmes. Their function is to establish relevance at a particular time and to encourage on-going work.

Situational morality involves, in William James' words, "moving away from abstraction and insufficiency, from verbal solutions, from bad a priori reasons, from ... closed systems ... towards concreteness and adequacy"[18].

Whether an individual develops the capacity for moral choice and the inclination to apply that choice depends, not on gene-dominated maturation or rational development alone, but on his total experience. We are responsible for that experience.

Notes

1 Kant, I., 'Groundwork of the Metaphysic of Morals', in The Moral Law, (trans. Paton, H.), Hutchinson, 1948.

2 Temple, W., Men's Creatrix, Macmillan, 1917, p. 206.

3 Erikson, E.H., 'The problem of ego identity', in Stein, M., et al. (eds.) Identity and Anxiety, Free Press, 1960.

4 Hare, R.M., The Language of Morals, Oxford University Press, 1952.

5 Wilson, J., Williams, N., and Sugarman, B., Introduction to Moral Education, Penguin, 1967.

6 Fletcher, J., Situation Ethics. The New Morality, SCM Press, 1966.

7 Durkheim, E., Moral Education. A Study of Theory and Application in the Sociology of Education, Free Press, 1961.

8 Piaget, J., The Moral Judgement of the Child, Routledge & Kegan Paul, 1932.

9 Kohlberg, L. and Turiel, E., Moralization Research, the Cognitive Approach, Holt, Rinehart and Winston, 1961.

10 McPhail, P., Ungoed-Thomas, J. and Chapman, H., Moral Education in the Secondary School, Longman, 1972.

11 Crawford, D.G. and Signori, E.I., 'An application of the critical incident technique to university teaching', Canadian Psychologist, vol. 3, no. 4, 1962; Flanagan, J.C., 'Leadership skills: their identification, development and evaluation', in Petrullo, L. and Bars, B. (eds.), Leadership and Interpersonal Behaviour, Holt, Rinehart and Winston, 1961.

12 McPhail, P., et al., Startline, Longman, 1978.

13 Ungoed-Thomas, J., The Moral Situation of Children, Macmillan, 1978.

14 Tinbergen, N., 'The importance of being playful', Times Educational Supplement, 10 January 1977.

15 Dickson, A., 'Altruism and action', Journal of Moral Education, vol. 8, no. 3, 1979.

16 McPhail, P., et al., Lifeline, Longman, 1972.

17 McPhail, P., et al., 1978 opcit.

18 James, W., 'What pragmatism means', in Selected Writings on Philosophy, Dent (Everyman edition), 1917, pp. 198-217.

The foregoing chapter was based on an article contributed by the author to a Special Number of the International Review of Education XXVI/1980/2, on the theme, 'Problems of Teaching Moral Values in a Changing Society'. Permission to use the article was kindly granted by the copyright holder, the Unesco Institute for Education, Hamburg.

Chapter 8

FIRST STEPS IN MORAL EDUCATION

John Wilson

For reasons which I hope to make clear towards the end of this chapter, I deem it prudent to approach my title obliquely. In certain areas or departments of life, not only do people vary dramatically in respect of their particular beliefs or values, but there is no general agreement on methodology – on how to handle the whole department. Also people are apt to invest a good deal of emotion. 'Ideological', perhaps 'controversial', may be fair, if fairly useless, titles for these. Examples might include morality, politics and religion. I want first to lay down criteria which have to be satisfied if we are to speak seriously of 'education' in these areas, and if we are actually to educate people in them. That sounds like a rather (as people are apt to say) 'abstract' or 'philosophical' approach to a notorious practical problem: but this appearance is misleading. For the main practical obstacles consist, as I see it, precisely in the facts that we either do not want to educate people in these areas, or despair of being able to do so. Once we get a clear grasp of what such education would look like in principle, the difficulties of putting it into practice are comparatively small.

It is worth noticing, as a preliminary encouragement, that there are several areas which might well be regarded as 'ideological' but (in general) are not, simply because educators have retained sufficient nerve and common sense to keep satisfactory educational practices going. Teachers of science have not, generally speaking (and long may this continue), been so unnerved by relativistically-minded philosophers of science like Kuhn[1] as to have serious doubts about the educational validity of their subject. One might think that to be because the central features of scientific methodology - what counts as 'doing science well' - were, in fact, tolerably clear. But it is also true that teachers of English literature and other aesthetic subjects continue to teach despite the fact that these areas, perhaps more than almost any other, present great difficulty to the methodologist. Just what does count as being 'good at literary criticism', or 'musical appreciation'? By what criteria do we - if indeed we do - judge some works of art better than others? What principles of reasons or standards of success do govern aesthetic matters? It is very hard to articulate, or even to be clear about, the answers to such questions: but there is notwithstanding, some confidence that in making certain practical moves in education - getting the pupils to note the development of character in a novel, or pick out the voices of a fugue, or whatever - we have a kind of tacit know-ledge of the answers.

I am not saying here that the mere existence of a practical consensus guarantees the right educational moves in these areas. I am saying rather that our tacit understanding of an area, when suitably clarified, may be quite sufficient to give us a satisfactory start provided - and with 'ideological' areas it is a big proviso - we are content to stay within the area and treat it for what it is. We get on fairly well with literature and music (generally speaking: I do not deny there are disputes) because we recognise tacitly what sort of business we are in. If somebody starts object-ing to the **literary** merits of P.G. Wodehouse because he broad-casted on behalf of the Nazis, or the **musical** merits of Beethoven because he was a bourgeois, we recognise that he is in a different business, the business of politics. This understanding protects us, though in these ideological days not infallibly, against this kind of confusion of categories.

I shall suggest that by 'educating pupils in X', where X is some department of life or form of thought, we should normally be taken to mean at least three things:

1. That we show the pupils the appropriate criteria of success for thinking and acting in this department or form, the way in which X comes within the scope of reason: in particular, what counts as relevant evidence for opinions and beliefs. In a word, we encourage them to be reasonable (perceptive, sane, knowledgeable, well-informed, etc.) in X. Not just **about** X: it is one thing to know a lot (as a historian or sociologist or whatever) **about** mathematics and religion, another thing to have learned to perform well **in** those departments.

2. That we can justify our title 'education in X' (rather than Y) only if we pay particular attention to what is peculiar to X as a department or form. Thus 'education in religion' would be, at best, a misleading title if all we did was to educate children in respect of certain historical or scientific facts (that happened, as it were contingently, to be connected with certain religions), or in the literary merits of certain religious documents.

3. That we should encourage the pupils to make up their own minds in X, by using the methodology or principles of reason appropriate to it, rather than (or anyway as well as) encouraging them to believe certain conclusions or 'right answers'.

These might all be argued to follow from what we mean by 'educate', via the connection of that term with what we mean by 'learn' (the notion of learning marks not just any change, but a change in the direction of truth by the application of reason and the use of evidence), and I have argued this elsewhere[2]. But in any case it seems that we are here talking about a coherent and worthwhile enterprise, whether or not it is the only enterprise meriting the title 'education'. Of course there may be those who do not wish to engage in this enterprise at all, perhaps because they are frightened of the possible outcome: with such I have no desire to argue here. The chances are that, in a pluralistic and shrinking world, such people will be driven willy-nilly to pay some attention to it: for instance, to allow **some** time for 'education in religion', in the above sense, even if they insist on using other time to inculcate certain specific religious beliefs and practices. My worry is more for those educators who would like to engage in this enterprise, but are unclear about how it can get off the ground. The main difficulty, I suspect, is that we only half-believe (at best) that the various titles - 'politics', 'morals', 'religion' and so on - can stand, or be made to stand, for distinguishable enterprises that are **about** something distinguishable and have some sort of distinguishable **point**. We see them rather as arenas in which various combatants do battle, providing amusement for sociologists and other empirical commentators but not otherwise engaged in any cooperative or constructive endeavour. That is certainly not an inevitable view: not only Plato and Aristotle but many of their successors saw at least some of them as enterprises with their own peculiar goods and virtues, somewhat on an analogy with the arts and crafts. Less apt to take anything as given, or more influenced by the variety both of particular ideologies and of conceptual systems which the study of history has displayed to us, we feel much more insecure: some philosophers going so far as to claim that the very concepts marked by 'politics', 'morality', etc. are 'contestable', thus putting everything at the service of ideology[3].

A more Kantian approach, however, may make us recover our senses. It is not difficult to see that there is, or might be, a sense of 'politics' such that (a) politics is inevitably (i.e. whatever one's preferences or 'values') an important human concern, and (b) politics, properly understood, contains within itself a number of non-disputable goods and virtues. Politics, we shall say, is an enterprise concerned with the good of associations or communities (**poleis**) as such. Not only the need for child-rearing but many other needs (the development of language, for instance, which cannot happen in isolation) makes this enterprise inevitable for human beings; and since human beings are always potentially vulnerable to each other, any man must necessarily have some concern with politics - how much, is another matter. At the same time, there will be certain necessarily desirable features of a community as such: justice, individual freedom, security, and good communications are amongst these. Anyone who rejected these as goods would have failed to understand what it was to be a human being, or what it was to be a member of a community: they are not ideological but logical goods, and the virtues that go with them are also logically required by the nature of the enterprise.

To make this sort of approach conceptually watertight would require much more philosophical argument than is appropriate here. But at least we can see that there are some logical necessities and some concepts which are inherent in politics, round which the pupils' understanding can legitimately be built, and that these have a very different status from particular ideologies, current practices, or 'values', that happen to be flying around. Thus the ideas marked by 'rules', 'sanctions', 'authority', 'contract', and many others are inalienable for men, and pupils need to get a firm grasp on them, not only a conceptual grasp, but the kind of grasp best given by practical participation and the taking of political responsibility (in particular, perhaps, taking the rap for bad decisions or arrangements). If we also give those pupils the attitudes, abilities and skills that are logically required for dealing appropriately with other people in any context - respect for other people's interests, emotional insight, determination and so forth – then the pupils will be equipped to think and act rationally in political contexts: and it will eventually be up to them to decide what practical realisations of the inalienable concepts they think best in this or that situation.

Nor is it difficult to distinguish this approach from one which more or less overtly recommends a particular set of political values. In our own sort of society the most tempting candidate is 'democracy', whatever this may mean; and it is moderately scandalous that most suggested programmes of political education incorporate 'democracy' in a way which takes its value for granted. Still more scandalous, if less naive, are attempts usually made tacitly to define 'politics' in such a way that other forms of government, oligarchy for instance, do not count as political at all. Such moves make it more difficult for pupils and teachers to raise the very important political question of whether 'democracy', in some or all of its senses, is actually a good thing: moves which are illegitimate from a strictly educational viewpoint, and ultimately impractical because sooner or later pupils will raise this question anyway.

'Health education' affords a similar illustration. Physical health presents comparatively little difficulty, because there is at least a central core of goods which are virtually undeniable – the free use of one's limbs, freedom from pain, and so on. (Though even here moral questions may come in: why not a short life and a merry one? I have not seen the idea of a rational attitude to one's body properly worked out in any health education courses.) But mental health requires the same treatment as politics. Either there is an undeniable central core here too, in which case we can at least show our pupils what it is, and educate them so that they understand and practise it: or else there is not, in which case there seems little point in imposing our own preferred mental styles on our pupils – since **ex hypothesi,** they are not ultimately grounded in reason.

Again, once we have made the distinction, we can easily list some features of such a core. That a man should recognise objective facts about the world, that he should be free from inner compulsion, that he should be as happy as the world allows him – these and other 'values' (and the uselessness of that word emerges in such contexts as this) are such that no reasons could be given for denying their general application. The non-disputable core of 'mental health' is incorporated in the general notion of rationality, as Richard Peters pointed out some time ago[4]. To be very sharply contrasted with this are more disputable and substantive notions like enjoying one's job (but one might be a slave), or being 'adjusted to society' (but one might live in Nazi Germany). The difference is clear enough; what we have to do is to work out the non-disputable core in more detail, and translate it into practical methods of education.

In these and some other cases we can see a way forward. But some areas, or at least their titles, present greater difficulty – a difficulty which relates to the second of my three principles mentioned above. In order to establish a viable and **sui generis** area of education, we need to be sure that our titles stand for something tolerably **distinctive.** We have to be able to distinguish – even though there may be overlaps – between matters of politics and matters of mental health, between politics and morality, between morality and religion. Most educators abandon this struggle, and are content to operate very general courses under some extremely vague heading – 'Learning to Live', 'Growing Up' or whatever. Even when the titles are not in themselves so vague, the actual practice may be: under 'religious education' all sorts of things may go on which have no distinctive connection with religion.

We may now be tempted to renege on our second principle:

for why should this distinctiveness matter? If we can cover all the relevant ground under the broad title of 'Learning to Live', what is the point of these philosophical or taxanomic exercises? But the trouble is that, without an effective taxonomy and set of categories, we cannot be sure that we **are** covering all the ground. These 'ideological areas' do exist, even though we may be unclear about them: there are important differences, even though they do not always appear in their titles. In a precisely similar way we could abolish the distinctions between school subjects or forms of thought, and run a succession of classroom periods all entitled 'Life' or 'The Environment'; but pretty soon we should have to think about just what the differences were between the various kinds of teaching and learning we might put under this heading.

The taxonomic difficulties with the word 'moral' are notorious, though even here I think it possible to distinguish a number of different enterprises in a strategically sensible way, thus freeing them for educators to put into practice. A better example for our purposes might be the idea of sex education. Insofar as this consists merely of biology or other empirical matters, it had better be classified as such. The real question is whether the notion of sexuality gives us a sufficiently distinctive area to justify a distinctive educational set of practices. Thus if one thought that, apart from the biology, anything worth doing under the title of 'sex education' really amounted to the education of emotions that were, in fact, common both to the the sexual arena and to all or most other arenas of life, then one might prefer to run courses under the title of 'the emotions' and bring in references to these arenas on the side (sex, friendship, the family, violence and so forth). If on the other hand one believed in specifically sexual emotions, then 'sex education' would stand for something sufficiently distinctive.

That may still seem no more than a matter of tactics of nomenclature; and certainly it raises the question of what the criteria of distinctiveness are to be. Must we identify a different form of thought, or a different set of goods and virtues? If we can, that might settle it: but there are many ongoing and successful sets of educational practices which use different criteria - many traditional subjects, for instance, are not distinctive in these ways. Might not a sufficient criterion be that pupils, and/or our present society, do in fact focus their concern on a certain area, marked by 'sex', or 'war', or whatever? That would justify any concern so focussed, and be the natural prey of fashion or ideology (Women's Studies, Black Studies, Disco Studies, and so forth). We want something more distinctive and less fragile than that. No doubt some compromise between different sets of criteria will have to be made, if only because some criteria are more connected with the pupils' motivation than others. But no compromise will solve our present problem: whatever headings we use, we still have to grapple (as do the pupils) with the question of whether there **is** something distinctive about 'sexuality' as an educational area, and if so what it is. We cannot avoid the task of getting the concepts clear, whatever we do with the titles.

In much the same way we need to know what may be distinctively put under the title of 'religion': what kind of truth (if any) **religious** truth is, as against the truths of history, morality and other enterprises. Having distinguished this, it is then indeed a tactical or pedagogic question of how best to organise our time - whether we should have separate periods specifically devoted to this distinctiveness, or whether we should allow it and other kinds of distinctiveness to emerge in the study of some general topic or field. But we have to distinguish it in the first place if we are to have anything worth calling 'education in religion' at all.

Simply to avoid the charge of indoctrination, or to tell the pupils something about religion (or, more commonly various particular creeds), is not good enough.

Educators in most liberal societies, at least recently, have been so anxious to avoid the charge of indoctrination that they have (generally speaking) failed even to confront these problems, let alone make a serious effort to solve them. Their continual and (so far as it goes) justifiable concern for 'neutrality', particularly if they are directly liable to the political pressures of a pluralist society with many articulate interest-groups (pressures which may deter them from even attempting certain 'hot' areas, such as sex and race), has encouraged them to duck the task. In this they have received much support from a relativistic climate of opinion, which would (I suppose) deny any sense to the idea of a pupil's becoming more reasonable, or perceptive, or well-educated in X as those terms are normally - that is transcendentally - used: 'reasonable' for relativists presumably means 'what this or that society takes to be reasonable'. (I say 'presumably' because the translation is obviously a wrong one, and it is hard to see how any English-speaker with his wits about him could offer it.)

It is very remarkable that, at a time when there is more discussion of the curriculum than perhaps ever before, educators are more than ever unwilling to ask the right questions: questions of the form 'Just what is X?' (where 'X' is the title or potential title for some subject, area or department), 'How is X different from Y and Z?', 'What is the point of X?', 'What is it to do X well?'. It is one thing to make a general, heterogeneous and high-sounding list of 'aims and objectives' and to attach them (tenuously) to a title: quite another to make the kind of distinctions we need in order to make sense not only of these 'ideological areas' but of the curriculum generally. Where there is already a satisfactory set of practices attached to a title, and provided (a big proviso) that educators are not swayed to change them by mere fashion, this may not too much matter: but where we have only a set of possible titles, as with the 'ideological areas', the only way forward is to try to make the right distinctions.

I incline to suspect (though this is no more than a sort of psychiatric guess - I hope, an 'educated' one) that the causes lie deeper than the desire to cling to one's own values or ideology on the one hand, or the despair of any non-relativistic application of reason on the other. These symptoms themselves perhaps indicate a more basic dislike, amounting (when philosophers press the point) to hatred and alarm, of making distinctions and categories in general. It is certainly no accident that our age puts a lot of money on the notion of 'integration', almost as if the mere existence of different categories or the mere fact of separateness and difference were threatening or otherwise intolerable. For consider what we should have to face, if and when we get the categories sorted out and properly understood. It would then appear that there were specific standards and criteria we had to meet in politics, morality, religion and the rest, if we wanted to be taken seriously, just as we have to meet them in doing mathematics or science: that some of us were very **bad** at politics, morality, etc., and others of us much more expert - so much more, perhaps, that the idea of entrusting political, moral, and other decisions to experts would no longer seem ridiculous: above all, that we could not any longer amuse and comfort ourselves by clinging to a set of 'values', or an 'ideology', in a highly general and monistic sort of way, because we should be under pressure to assign different 'values' to different categories, where they would come under the scope of rigorous discipline - just as we cannot now respectably claim to have 'the truth', in empirical matters, across the board of all the empirical disciplines: for we recognise that truth in mathematics, science, history and other disciplines is **different.**

In the above I have been deliberately brief, and deliberately avoided any direct or sophisticated attack upon those philosophers who, in a way rightly, would challenge me at a good many points. I say 'in a way' because, whilst it is very important that the taxonomising and working out of these areas should be very carefully inspected and criticised, it is equally important that all those concerned should **want** to get the best answers we can: and I sense this desire to be often absent. Yet until we have equipped our selves at least with a plausible set of views about what a sensible taxonomy would look like, and what the criteria of reason or success actually are for each X in each category, it seems largely a waste of time to study the curriculum from the viewpoint of sociology or any other empirical discipline - if we have no clear grasp of what we are trying to do or where we are trying to move towards, we cannot even know **what** empirical facts are relevant. Does not much - perhaps almost all - of the study of 'curriculum innovation' depend on just what 'innovations' one should be trying to introduce? Social science may not even help us much to identify the opposition unless we first know what it is opposition **to.**

Perhaps I may be forgiven for offering an autobiographical, but I hope sufficiently paradigmatic, example. Fifteen years of trying to persuade educators that there is a set of attributes, demanded by pure reason, which any serious person concerned with 'morality' in at least one sense of the term ought to have, and ought to encourage pupils to have, has let me (tardily, I fear) to appreciate the strength and nature of resistance to any such idea[5]. Very often, if one simply lists these attributes, explains each, and shows why each is demanded by reason, such resistance will be very sharp. But if one adopts the strategy of asking educators to make their own list of attributes - to put down what, if anything, they honestly believe is required by reason for any serious moral thinker and agent - it nearly always turns out that the list they make is more or less identical (give or take a bit of terminology) both with the one I originally put forward and each other's. That is hardly surprising, if (as I believe) the items on such a list are tolerably obvious and require no immense intellectual talent to discern. What is more surprising is the intense dislike of being told, of any suggestion of 'authority', even if the authority has got it right. That may be a powerful argument for giving teachers and other educators much more autonomy, for putting them on the spot and getting them to face the right questions themselves, rather than react to the pressures of others. If they did, they might find what I have said above to be of some initial assistance.

I hope it will now be clearer why I spent so much time dealing with areas other than, or at least not more than overlapping with moral education. The reasons are (1) the exact area properly to be covered by that title is in dispute, and it is worth noticing that the inclusion or exclusion of other areas ('health education', 'political education', 'religious education', etc.) does not affect the central points relevant for dealing with any such area: it seems to me - comparatively - unimportant what titles are used, provided all the important areas are covered under some title or other ('value education' is popular in North America, for instance); more importantly, perhaps, (2) the first steps in any serious attempt at moral education must (as I see it) be the acceptance of the very few, and I think boringly obvious, basic points I have been advancing. Once that has happened, as it demonstrably has not in any country or culture of which I am aware, it is a very short step to (a) getting clearer about the objectives (surely along the lines I have repetitively suggested elsewhere, but make no apology for repeating yet again as an appendix here), (b) using one's common sense and imagination in devising and putting into practice those methods which either seem likely to achieve, or are logically required for achieving, these objectives, and (c) calling upon conceptually sophisticated psychologists and sociologists, if any can be found, to give us those hidden empirical facts which are relevant to our enterprise.

Until it has happened, we shall continue to deceive ourselves with activities or pseudo-activities which do no more than create the illusion of rational effort. Thus we may (as with most practical projects) do no more than encourage or stimulate discussion about morals or 'values', without giving our pupils any methodological guidance, any clear idea about **how** they are to decide which answers are right (indeed even suggesting by our silence that there are no such things as right answers to moral questions at all) or what considerations are relevant. We may retreat from the whole question of what it is to educate pupils specifically in morals by treating morality as some kind of fringe benefit to other parts of the curriculum - in particular, perhaps, to literature or history: we may even, I fear, use some such phrase as 'the ethical dimension of the curriculum' to avoid facing the key questions. (Nobody talks about 'the mathematical dimension of the curriculum', because we know how to teach mathematics.) We may set up yet more practical or 'development' projects, or units to assess moral performance, without having cleared the conceptual ground first: rather as some of us may live to see the 365th project on R.E., which like the previous 364 produces new and 'relevant' materials but entirely fails.

APPENDIX

Full List of Moral Components

PHIL(HC)	Having the concept of a 'person'.
PHILL(CC)	Claiming to use this concept in an overriding, prescriptive, universalised (O,P and U) principle.
PHIL(RSF) (DO & PO)	Having feelings which support this principle, either of a 'duty-oriented' (DO) or a 'person-oriented' (PO) kind.
EMP(HC)	Having the concepts of various emotions (Moods, etc.).
EMP(1)(Cs)	Being able, in practice to identify emotions, etc., in oneself, when these are at a conscious level.
EMP(1)(Ucs)	Ditto, when the emotions are at an unconscious level.
EMP(2)(Cs)	Ditto, in other people, when at a conscious level.
EMP(2)(Ucs)	Ditto, when at an unconscious level.
GIG(1)(KF)	Knowing other ('hard') facts relevant to moral decisions.
GIG(1)(KS)	Knowing sources of facts (where to find out) as above.
GIG(2)(VC)	'Knowing how': a 'skill' element in dealing with moral situations, as evinced in verbal communication with others.
GIG(2)(NVC)	Ditto, in non-verbal communication.
KRAT(1)(RA)	Being, in practice, 'relevantly alert' to (noticing) moral situations, and seeing them as such (describing them in terms of PHIL, etc. above).
KRAT(1)(TT)	Thinking thoroughly about such situations, and bringing to bear whatever PHIL, EMP, and GIG one has.

KRAT(1)(OUP)   As a result of the foregoing, making an over-riding, prescriptive and universalised decision to act in others' interests.

KRAT(2)   Being sufficiently whole-hearted , free from unconscious counter-motivation, etc. to carry out (when able) the above decision in practice.

These 'components' ('constituents', 'necessary features', 'pieces of equipment', or whatever it's best to call them) are of course **logical** and not **empirical**. I mean that they are simply an expansion of what it **means to be** 'educated in morality', what characteristics are required by logic. They are not mental forces or entities of any kind. They represent the (only proper) objectives for any attempt on moral education, independent of class or culture or any other empirical feature. In similar ways, presumably a (logical) list of attributes forming what we mean by 'a good scientist' or 'a well-educated' historian' could be produced (though I am not aware of any very satisfactory lists of this sort) – and would need to be, if we were to be really clear about the objectives of teaching science or history.

Notes

1   Kuhn, T.S., The Structures of Scientific Revolutions, University of Chicago Press, 1962.

2   Wilson, J., Philosophy of Education, Routledge & Kegan Paul, 1979.

3   Hartnett, A., and Naish, M., Theory and Practice of Education, Heinemann, 1976.

4   Peters, R.S., 'Mental health as an educational aim', in Hollins, T.H.B., (ed.) The Aims of Education, Manchester University Press, 1964.

5   Wilson, J., A Teacher's Guide to Moral Education, Geoffrey Chapman, 1973.

Chapter 9

PERSONAL AND SOCIAL EDUCATION

Richard Pring

1 Introduction

Professor Lawton has written of the need in any curriculum for a common core of experiences and of learning objectives which would be a fair balance between the different activities that compete for a place on the timetable. And such a balance would be not between subjects only, because there are many worthwhile things to be learnt that cannot be easily fitted into traditional subjects. Nor must such a balance be seen in terms of different kinds of knowledge. Feelings, emotions, behaviour, activities also can be learnt, modified, and refined. Rather must we think of the impact of the curriculum as a whole upon the values, understandings, activities and behaviour of the pupils. And it follows that we must do some curriculum planning across the curriculum – across the subject boundaries which are the most significant feature of most schools' curricula[1].

Particularly is this true where the curriculum takes on board, not only maths or physics or history, but also personal and social education. Firstly, all that happens in different parts of the curriculum has some impact upon the sort of person that the pupil becomes. Secondly, however, personal development cannot be reduced to what is contained within these different parts. There is a need, therefore, to be aware of the effects on more deeply personal development of what is being done in maths, history or any subject, whilst at the same time having in mind the many other things which **ought** to be going on somewhere in the curriculum if pupils are to develop as persons in a socially defensible way.

In this paper I want to do two things. First I want to point to some of the philosophical problems in this way of thinking. Secondly, I want to indicate how one might proceed practically in thinking across the curriculum in the light of these philosophical considerations.

2 Context

Schools have always been concerned with the personal and social education of pupils – whether this be called character training or pastoral care or the formation of moral values. Often, of course, it is implicit in a way of life, a set of rules, and the relationships that are fostered between pupil and teacher. It has in recent years become part of the curriculum directly through tutorial periods[2] and other aspects of the 'pastoral system' of the school – or, of course, indirectly through the treatment of certain topics in the humanities, religious education, or social studies. Any subjects that deal with personal, social and moral values, as in literature, are contributing to the personal and social development of pupils. Very recently, however, a concern for personal and social education, and the need to place it more centrally on the curriculum, has been expressed in various reports and initiatives. Briefly, I want to point out the following:

(a) HMI report A View of the Curriculum[3]: 'personal and social development in the broad sense (' ... prepared to meet the basic intellectual and social demands of adult life, and helped to form an acceptable set of personal values ... ' etc.) is a major charge on the curriculum'.

(b) HMI Secondary Survey (in a chapter devoted entirely to personal and social development) 'In recent years, these major objectives (viz. opportunities and experiences ... that will help their personal development as well as preparing them for the next stage of their lives) have assumed a more significant and conscious place in the aspirations of schools in response to external pressures and to changes in society, and within the schools themselves'.

(c)   The Consultative Document Education in Schools gives as the third major aim of education: 'to instil respect for moral values, for other people and for oneself, and tolerance of other races, religions and ways of life.'

(d)   HMI document Curriculum 11 to 16 picked out, in its check-list for a balanced common curriculum, three areas 'the ethical', 'the social and political', and the 'spiritual'.

(e)   The Assessment of Performance Unit's comprehensive mapping of the whole curriculum contained, as one of its six areas, personal and social development[4].

(f)   The Further Education Unit at the DES has placed at the centre of its curriculum for vocational preparation various aspects of personal and social education, often referred to as 'Social and Life Skills'[5].

Indeed it is worth pointing out that, in the few studies undertaken to find out what most of all is required of pupils when they leave school, employers and others put at the top of their list of desirable moral and personal attributes, qualities such as 'responsibility' for actions, for consequences of actions and for decisions which affect themselves and others[6]. Educating pupils to accept responsibility for what they are and do may be one of the most important of curriculum aims.

There are, too, social problems that we face which are making new demands upon the personal education of pupils. It is, of course, both easy and mistaken to place the responsibility for vandalism, violence, or racial hatred upon schools. Rather it is the case that, in areas where there is such anti-social behaviour, schools so often remain one of the few oases of humane and civilized life (police in Toxteth and Brixton might learn a lesson or two from how schools cope with the local lads – teachers, whatever their problems, have not yet had to be issued with riot shields or C.S. Gas[7]). Nonetheless, schools cannot remain indifferent to these social disturbances and need to think how they might educate pupils for a more tolerant and responsible role in a rather disturbed society.

3 Problems

There are considerable difficulties however in translating this general concern into curriculum terms. These might be categorised as follows:

(a) Values

Central to our concern about personal and social education must be the values that pupils acquire and that guide their behaviour. But immediately there are problems. There seems on the surface to be so little agreement in our society over what should be held valuable in life or what are one's rights and obligations. Furthermore, it is frequently argued that there is no **objective** way of sorting out these differences – they are a matter of taste or they are relative to different social and individual interests. Furthermore, so it is argued, no one has the right 'to impose' one set of values upon another.

I cannot here meet this objection in detail. I would, however, like to make three points. Firstly, there is more consensus over basic principles than is often assumed. Thus, most people would agree that injuring people for the sheer pleasure of it, cruelty to children, stealing personal belongings, and so on are wrong. We note the differences between people in the values they hold, but often take for granted so much that binds them together. Secondly, differences in value are not simply a matter of taste. There is such a thing as moral argument and moral reasoning. Most people who reflect on their values do, in the light of various considerations pointed out to them, change their views over a period of time. Most people are open to persuasion in the light of relevant considerations. Thirdly, however, 'values education' is something that one cannot opt out of – one is, as a parent or teacher, inevitably caught up in it, encouraging certain kinds of relationships rather than others, fostering certain kinds of interests, etc.

Nonetheless, the scepticism that some hold over the possibility of rationally resolving value issues has had its curriculum consequences. An interesting development in the United States is the teaching of 'values clarification'[8] – not promoting one set of values rather than another, but enabling pupils to sort out what their values are.

(b) **Conceptual**

To say that personal and social education has at its centre a concern for values only takes us a small way towards sorting out what it is. The main difficulty (and certainly the overriding problem in curriculum planning) lies in the vast territory that is subsumed under it. Presumably the English teacher introducing Middlemarch, the history teacher dealing with the social consequences of the Civil War, the R.E. teacher explaining various religious ideals, the house tutor helping a pupil through some emotional difficulty, the P.E. teacher persuading the rugger team to grit their teeth in the face of fierce opposition – all would claim with justification to be contributing to the personal and social development of the pupils. How can one make coherent curriculum sense out of such a wide range of classroom activities, teaching objectives, sought-for skills, attitudes, habits, values?

(c) **Political**

The distinction between personal and social values is not clearcut – the sort of person one is affects indirectly the sort of social relationships that develop and vice versa. By helping the child to develop certain personal values one is inevitably affecting the sort of society that we are to live in. One could, but need not, refer to the influence of the personal values and relationships fostered by the public school ethos upon the prevailing values in society and the way in which society is organised and run. Attitudes to authority developed through the education a pupil receives in school will have their spin-off later in life when confronted by the decisions of other authorities. To that extent, those teachers therefore who accept some measure of responsibility for personal and social education of young people inevitably raise questions about the sort of society they are being educated for. And this makes this area of education of political significance. The HMI paper Curriculum 11-16 is aware of the possible clash between economic demands made upon schools (preparing them for the world of work etc.) and the personal values (of critical reflection, say) which teachers may be keen to develop. Perhaps an efficiently run society does not want too many people who have minds and purposes of their own.

4 Being a Person

To begin to reduce this vast and controversial area to some manageable size, and thus to map out the territory for curriculum purposes, we need to attend initially to what it is to be a person - and thus to enable people to develop as persons or to treat and respect them as persons or to educate them in those aspects of their being which are central to being a person. Rather dogmatically, I suggest the following features of being a person:

(i) A person is an object that you can see, touch, and smell, that you can push, measure and weigh. In that respect, a person is like any other physical object.

(ii) But persons, not mere physical objects, have a form of consciousness. To be conscious of things requires some set of concepts through which experience is ordered and made sense of.

(iii)   Part of a person's conceptual repertoire is the concept
of 'person' - he sees others as persons, having their own
ideas etc., and this enables him to relate to others
meaningfully. Furthermore, his concept of person comes to
be applied to himself - there is the capacity for reflection
and self-awareness.

(iv)   Persons are not conscious of things in a purely passive sense
like a camera receiving snapshots of the world outside.
They react to the world in a purposeful way. Persons act
intentionally, and we typically explain their behaviour in
terms, not of causes, but of their intentions.

(v)   Persons acting intentionally are the bearers of moral attributes. We praise or blame them, respect them, hold them
more or less responsible for what they do.

By the time children reach school they are recognizably
persons - with a developed form of consciousness, recognising
others as persons and relating to them in a meaningful way,
acting intentionally, and the subject of moral appraisal. But it is
educationally important to ask whether one can talk of them
becoming more fully a person or developing as persons. There
does seem to be a good reason for thinking in these terms, and if
this is true there is ample opportunity for detailed curriculum
thinking.

First, a young child has a concept of 'person' in some minimal
sense, as is reflected in the personal relationships it has with
parents. This early ability however to pick out objects as persons
and to relate to them as persons is in itself in need of development. For example, although a young child shows through his
behaviour that he recognises others as persons (having a form of
conscious life, emotions, intentions etc.), he does not realise that
such intentions and feelings might be different from his own[9]. It

is the absence of this ability which Piaget refers to as ego-centrism - and of course, as in any changing psychological cap-acity, the transition from ego-centrism to altruism is gradual[10].

Secondly, one can have the concept of a 'person' but, through lack of imagination or through not having grasped it fully, fail to apply it as widely as one should - to blacks, young children, women, heathens (history gives us many lessons in this).

Thirdly, connected with this developing sophistication of per-sonal understanding is a qualitative change in the sort of relation-ships that one person can have with another - from the rather instrumental relationships at the ego-centric stage through the role relationships where one sees others to be particular sorts of persons, to the close personal relationships at the stage when another's different and individual point of view can be recognised and respected[11].

Fourthly, there is a gradual development of those concepts to do with intentions, motives, responsibility, etc. which enable one to describe and appraise others and oneself in an adequate per-sonlike way. It is quite a sophisticated exercise to explain some-one's behaviour in terms of motives such as ambition or jealousy.

Fifthly, not only do the relevant forms of consciousness dev-elop, in terms of which one can recognise others and relate to them as persons, but so do the ways we can be said to act responsibly. People are more or less responsible for what they do. We excuse people the full penalty of their crimes because of mitigated responsibility or extenuating circumstances. Especially is this the case with young children, and indeed with adolescents. Only gradually are we prepared to ascribe full responsibility for their actions, and for determining their own future. To be res-ponsible for what one does and for one's own destiny is part of what we mean by being a person but is only slowly achieved - and some, one might observe, never really achieve it. This is a difficult notion to sort out in detail, but it underlies the frequent reference to 'autonomy' as an educational ideal and as the proper end of personal development[12]. By autonomy is meant self-determination or control over one's own life and decisions. It is contrasted with the situation in which someone is not master of his own situation, but whose life is the product of influences or forces or desires or emotions over which he has little control.

Finally, there are certain intellectual or conceptual developments which seem basic to recognising others and relating to them as persons, as well as to acting responsibly. This is the capacity to see events in terms of fairness and impartiality. It is interesting to see how this capacity is something that only slowly emerges, affecting how one sees and relates to different people.

Such a brief indication of what could be **meant** by development in a person may seem hopelessly abstract, but it does suggest practically relevant questions that should be directed at the impact of the curriculum upon pupils – certain general criteria against which the curriculum as a whole might be tested. Does the curriculum, for example,

(i)   respect pupils as persons, centres of consciousness, capable of contributing to the various explorations, enquiries, or activities that children and adults engage in?

(ii) assist pupils to see others (e.g. ethnic minorities) as persons in the sense described?

(iii) enable pupils to see themselves as persons in this sense, and as such worthy of self-respect and the respect of others?

(iv) encourage that independence of thought, that systematic reflective thinking, which is the proper life of a self-conscious being?

We must however distinguish between such general character-istics of being a person and more specific ones – those of being a person of a particular sort. To hold up this or that sort of person as the ideal to be encouraged seems much more relative to the particular values that one holds, or the kind of society that one would like to foster. Some schools attach importance to punctuality, obedience, and conformity, emphasising sex differences through clubs, games, and wearing of uniforms. The reasons for such practices, if made explicit, would reflect the ideas which the school had for proper growth as a person (at least for these little persons) or for the sort of society they would like to bring about.

If we were to set about developing through the curriculum the **sort** of person of our dreams, what kind of qualities or powers would we aim to teach and thus to make explicit in our planning? The following list of **categories** might help one to decide:

(i) intellectual virtues: these are the dispositions such as concern for getting at the truth which are characteristic of persons engaged in intellectual enquiry. Presumably the teacher of history must see as essential to the activity a respect for evidence in arriving at conclusions, and therefore would want to engender this respect in the pupils.

(ii) moral virtues: these are dispositions such as kindness and patience which control the feelings. Different people do have different emotional dispositions, and what should go into a list of those to be encouraged would not necessarily get universal agreement. Tolerance is a virtue cherished by the English liberal but not by the Iranian mullah. What are virtues for some (e.g. modesty, humility, thrift) may for others be vices. And different schools do seem to encourage different kinds of dispositions - through the relationships, activities and rules of the school.

(iii) Character traits: these are qualities of the 'will' such as perseverance or courage. Hitler may not have been very

virtuous but unfortunately he had a strong character. Very
often certain curriculum activities, such as playing tough
games in rough weather, have been defended because they
are supposed to strengthen the character

(iv)   Social competencies: these could include the ability to deal
with certain kinds of social situations, such as chatting
amiably to strangers or entertaining friends. But it could
also include basic good manners, for example, giving up
one's seat to the elderly, infirm or pregnant. The boundary between morality and etiquette is blurred in places
although too much importance is often attached to the
relatively trivial.

(v)   practical knowledge: we often assess a person in terms of
practical abilities – he is a 'practical person', meaning
that in a wide range of practical tasks such as repairing
cars or DIY jobs in the home he can generally solve
problems and display intelligence. Or we refer to someone
as a political person, meaning that he has a quick practical
grasp of political situations and can deal shrewdly with
certain kinds of interpersonal problems.

(vi)   theoretical knowledge: one cannot ignore, in spelling out
the sort of person someone should become, the understandings, concepts, beliefs, insights that are afforded
through theoretical study. Being a person, as opposed to a
mere object, presupposes some developed form of consciousness, but that form of consciousness can be developed in
different ways. A 'religious person' must have certain
religious concepts and understandings. Deny him these and
he would not be that sort of person.

(vii)   personal values: two equally virtuous people (see (i) and
(ii) above) might nonetheless disagree on what to value –
pacifism, for example, or private property. And it is char-

acteristic of the documents referred to earlier that teachers are exhorted to help children formulate their personal values without determining what these should be.

5 Mapping the Territory

I said at the beginning that the area is vast and that one needs, in the light of basic principles, to give it some shape and to define it in terms that make curriculum sense. The following is an attempt to map the territory as a result of the points and distinctions I have just made. This, however, can be no more than a sort of checklist, a guide to school-based curriculum discussion and planning. One should keep in mind both the general questions posed above. But this matrix below does alert us to the fact that personal and social education

(i)   must be concerned as much with values, dispositions, attitudes etc. as it is with the more cognitive aspect of development; and

(ii) the more general characteristics of being a person that I have talked about need to be expressed through more specific areas of knowing or behaving.

	Cognitive Capacity	Facts to be known	Attitudes, Feelings, Dispositions	Practical Application
A General Considerations Being a person (including the capacity for entering into personal relations)				
Moral perspective				
Ideals (including religious and other styles of life)				
B Specific Application Social issues - race - sexism - environment (e.g. political)				
Politics - citizenship - community participation - the law				
Place within society - career - economic needs				
Health - physical - mental				

Notes:

(a)   Cognitive Capacity - this includes reasoning ability, understanding, acquisition of relevant concepts.

(b)   Practical Application - how a person actually behaves, the
habits of behaving he has acquired, the skills of performing
in a certain way (these are distinguishable sub-categories).

(c)   Not all the cells need be filled - there may be no specific
moral facts to be known - only a certain cognitive capacity, relevant attitudes, etc., and certain habits.

Such a matrix is crude, unfinished, and merely suggestive, but
it sets out a framework within which one might work out in a
fairly coherent manner the individual kinds of knowledge, understanding, feelings, habits and skills which might enter into a
school's attempt to take seriously the personal and social
education of its pupils. Each school would need to fill in the cells
of the matrix with its own 'interpretation' of these fairly general
categories of knowledge or dispositions or practical application.

I am not suggesting, however, that such a filled-in matrix
would constitute a set of objectives to which one would teach
directly, - nor am I in any way advocating that such a mapped-
out area of curriculum concern should be treated as a subject on
the timetable. Many of these components of being a person or of
being a person of a particular sort (knowledgeable about certain
social issues which are important, having certain moral qualities
or dispositions, able to participate in certain aspects of practical
life, etc.) are acquired through the relationships that are
encouraged between teachers and pupils or through the content of
a particular subject or through a mode of teaching or through
extra-mural activities or through residential experiences. But one
ought to have some **detailed** account of what personal and social
development consists of, and one ought to be able to expose this
to the professional scrutiny of one's colleagues. Then one is able

to see where it is happening on the curriculum and what special arrangements need to be made to ensure there are no important gaps.

Indeed, in order to fill these gaps, there may be a need for the school to engage in its own research project – to find out what, for instance, are the 'survival skills' required by people living within that community or what personal qualities are judged to be most important to local employers (but often lacking in the applicants). Already there are teaching materials, teaching strategies such as simulation exercises and role play, which are geared to the development of personal and social qualities, and these too need to be explored within the curriculum framework developed by the school.

Such a mapping of the territory, therefore should be treated much more as a logically defensible check list of the different components that might enter into one's analysis of personal and social education. It might also be the basis of a more generous profile of the pupil's achievements during and at the end of schooling. Too often we give through our reports, examinations and assessments, a very inadequate picture of this rather complex person because we do not attend to those many important factors which make him the sort of person he is and which result, at least in part, from the influences of the school.

Notes

1 This chapter is a development (and therefore incorporates part) of a paper given at the Cambridge Institute of Education and published in the Cambridge Journal of Education, vol. 11, no. 2, 1981. The chapter arises out of criticism of the latter paper, especially of the Matrix.

2 See particularly the work of Button, L., Developmental Group Work with Adolescents, University of London Press, 1974; and the application of this in Baldwin, J. and Wells, H., Active Tutorial Work Book, 1 to 5, Blackwell, 1979.

3 This and the following three reports are

HMI, A View of the Curriculum, H.M.S.O., 1979.

HMI, Aspects of Secondary Education in England, H.M.S.O., 1979.

DES, Education in Schools: A Consultative Document, H.M.S.O., 1977.

HMI, Curriculum 11 to 16, D.E.S., 1977.

4 See Kay, B., 'Monitoring School Performance', in Trends in Education, 1975.

5 See F.E.U., Developing Social and Life Skills, D.E.S., 1980.

6 See Social and Applied Psychology Units, University of Sheffield, Young People Starting Work.

7 A point made at the time by Professor E. Wragg.

8 See Raths, L.E., and others, Values and Teaching: Working with Values in the Classroom, Merrill, 1978.

9 See Flavell, J.H., 'The Development of Inference about Others', in Mischel, T., (ed.), Understanding Other Persons, Blackwell, 1974.

10 See Piaget, J., The Language and Thought of the Child, Routledge, 1926.

11 Peters, R.S., 'Personal Understanding and Personal Relationships', and Secord, P.F., and Peevers, B.H., 'The Development and Attributes of Person Concepts', both in Mischel, T., op.cit.

12 See Dearden, R.F., 'Autonomy and Education', in Dearden, R.F., and others, Education and the Development of Reason, Routledge and Kegan Paul, 1972.

Chapter 10

THE ETHICAL VALUE OF RELIGIOUS EDUCATION

Jean Holm

Religious education is frequently equated with moral education or with personal and social education. In many secondary schools, after the third year, pupils have health education, moral education or careers guidance under the subject label 'religious education', and even DES and Schools Council documents sometimes deal with religious education in terms of 'spiritual and moral values'. It is important, therefore, to clarify what I mean by religious education before discussing the contribution which it can make to the ethical dimension of the curriculum.

The subject has undergone two main changes in direction in the past two decades, and in different ways each of the three approaches has been related to moral education.

The first approach is that of traditional RE, associated with the 1944 Education Act and the Agreed Syllabuses which were produced in the forties and fifties, though of course it stretches much further back into the history of education in Britain. The aim of traditional religious education was confessional, i.e. its concern was to teach for belief. Teaching was done within a context of commitment, taking for granted such things as the existence of God – the God whom Christians worship – and the divinity of Jesus. The content was mainly biblical but the aim, interestingly enough, was primarily moral. A large part of each syllabus was devoted to Jesus' teaching, particularly the parables, as guidance for the pupils' lives. The emphasis was on personal conduct rather than on the way in which people should behave in social and internation affairs, largely in terms of reward for obedience: God 'looked after' those who were 'good' - Noah, Abraham, Moses, David, Elijah, Daniel ... .

This emphasis on morality is partly explained by the nature of the debate which preceded the 1944 Act. Most of the advocates of the statutory provision of Religious Instruction in schools in Britain argued in terms of the need to stem the moral decline in society. (One finds similar arguments being used today by some of the more reactionary individuals and organisations who are campaigning for religious education to consist mainly of the teaching of the Christian faith.)

The first main change in the subject came in the sixties. It was part of the whole movement towards experience-based learning which followed the educational psychologists' demonstration of the importance of experience in the learning process. In religious education it took the form of life themes in the primary school and problem-centred discussion in the secondary school, at least from the age of 13 onwards.

Although its critics often accused this kind of religious education of being humanist, it was actually still confessional. This can be illustrated from the work of Harold Loukes, one of the pioneers of experience-based RE in the secondary school. He described his research into the effectiveness of religious education with young school leavers in a book called Teenage Religion[1], but his next book, suggesting how the subject could be handled more effectively, and advocating discussion of the kind of ethical issues which were important to adolescents, was called New Ground in Christian Education[2].

An often quoted aim for religious education in the sixties was to help children to 'find a faith to live by'[3]. Teachers saw their purpose as helping their pupils to choose between a religious and a non-religious interpretation of life, which meant in those days between Christianity and Humanism. Ironically, it was primarily the discussion of ethical issues which was used to help the pupils to make their choice – ironically, because I don't know any ethical issue in which all Humanists are ranged on one side and all Christians on the other. Many teachers, sensitive to the charge of indoctrination which had been levelled at traditional religious education, described their approach as 'open-ended', but as ethical issues tended to be discussed in relation to biblical passages, especially the teaching of Jesus, it is not surprising that most pupils believed that the dice were loaded in favour of Christianity.

This more subtle, and often unconscious, form of confessionalism was reflected in the widely used expression 'the religious dimension of life' – an expression which also betrays the lack of clear thinking which characterised discussion about religious education in this period. What is the religious dimension of a religious person's life? If a person is religious, then the whole of his life should be seen from a religious perspective. If a person has consciously rejected religion, then it is both illogical and discourteous to insist that he has a religious dimension to his life.

It was in the late sixties that we became more aware that we were living in a multi-faith society – a belated recognition, because there has been a Jewish community in Britain for centuries – and some, though not all, teachers realised how odd it was to use the teaching of Jesus, which has authority only for Christians, to help Hindu and Muslim and Sikh and Jewish pupils to behave more morally or to decide between a religious and a non-religious interpretation of life.

Many secondary religious education teachers, frustrated by an approach which involved discussing ethical issues in the light of biblical passages, welcomed the two Schools Council projects: on Moral Education (directed by Peter McPhail, and dealing mainly with personal relationships), and the Humanities (directed by Lawrence Stenhouse, and dealing with controversial social issues), and the wholesale use of the projects' materials in religious education ensured an even closer identification of the subject with moral education.

It was in the sixties that the name of the subject was changed from religious knowledge, religious instruction, divinity, scripture or whatever, to religious education. That was an important move, but it was not without its problems. Physical education aimed to improve pupils' physique, health education to make them healthier, moral education (in most people's minds) to make them more moral; was the purpose of religious education to make them more religious? The legacy of this confusion is still with us.

The second major change in the subject came at the beginning of the seventies, in response to the challenge which the philosophers of education issued to teachers – the challenge to justify what was being taught as a good educational experience for all pupils. For the purposes of this chapter the most significant feature of the analyses of the curriculum which the philosophers offered us, whether one followed Paul Hirst's forms of knowledge or Philip Phenix's realms of meaning, was the very clear distinction which was made between the religious and moral elements of the curriculum, and the justification of the inclusion of a study of religion as part of pupils' general education.

The aim which was developed in the seventies approach to religious education, and which has been adopted in one form or another by many of the new Agreed Syllabuses, is 'to help pupils to understand, by the time they leave secondary school, what religion is and what is means to take a religion seriously'.

There are three main differences between this kind of religious education and the two approaches which preceded it. First, it is not confessional; its aim is not to teach for belief. The approach is objective. 'Objective' does not mean, as is sometimes assumed, cold, clinical, detached; it means that the teacher is not offering value judgements about particular religions, or trying to persuade the pupils to accept the beliefs of one religion.

Secondly, it focuses on living religions. Traditional RE was Bible-based and, apart from forays into stories of such people as Augustine of Canterbury and David Livingstone and Elizabeth Fry, it was mainly concerned with what happened between three and two thousand years ago. And although the RE of the sixties dealt with issues which were considered relevant to the experience of the pupils, it still referred back to the Bible for support for moral behaviour. If, on the other hand, one wants to help pupils to understand the nature of religion, then one must study religions in their contemporary form. This will obviously involve some looking back to origins and developments in history, especially at secondary level, but the main focus will be on religions as they are practised today.

Thirdly, the content of the syllabus is wider than it used to be. It includes the study of more than one religion. Quite apart from the need to know something about the religions and cultures of the ethnic minorities who are part of our society, an understanding of religion as a human phenomenon requires some study of particular religions. Without this it is all too easy to assume that certain concepts or emotions or practices have the same central position in all religions.

What contribution, then, can be made to the ethical dimension of the curriculum by religious education when it takes the form of the study of religion?

It increases understanding of people from different religious and cultural backgrounds, thus removing one of the causes of intolerance and prejudice. It helps pupils to understand the place of morality in religion and in non-religious systems of belief –

the relationship between belief and life. It makes a contribution to pupils' understanding of the way in which moral judgements are made, and especially to their understanding of the complexity of moral issues. And it makes a contribution to their development as whole persons, able to be actively concerned with the welfare of others.

In illustrating these contributions I am necessarily selecting those aspects of religious education which are relevant to the theme of this book; I am not attempting to give a comprehensive description of the subject[4].

I want to look at three main areas:

the study of the phenomena of religions

the acquiring of skills needed for the study of religion

the exploration of experience.

First, then, the **study of the phenomena of religions.** This is quite different from the old-style comparative study of religion which many people will have experienced in their sixth form days: the rapid gallop through several world religions, with the emphasis on those things which distinguish them from each other. The aim of religious education which I am discussing is not to help pupils to understand **religions,** but to help them understand the **nature of religion.** Of course religion does not exist in a vacuum, and it can be seen only in the form of particular religions, but the emphasis will be on learning about the different elements which make up religion, and it is only in the upper part of the secondary school that these elements should be brought together in an attempt to gain an overall picture of a religion.

The temptation in Britain is to interpret religion too narrowly. Teachers belong to that section of society which thinks of religion mainly in terms of beliefs and morals. This is part of our Western, protestant, middle class heritage. For most other Christians, especially the Eastern Orthodox Church and Roman Catholicism in many parts of the world, and for all the other religions, especially Judaism, Hinduism and traditional - tribal religions, religion is far more than beliefs and morals. It is the whole framework of life within which a person grows up. It includes worship, and the buildings used for worship, and places of pilgrimage. It includes festivals. It includes scriptures and other sacred writings. It includes religious institutions, local as well as national or international. It includes rites and customs, particularly those associated with the rites of passage - the actions performed and the words spoken at the crisis moments of human life: birth, initiation, marriage and death.

These different elements or aspects of religion make up an important part of the agenda of religious education. Pupils need to start, as in other areas of the curriculum, with the concrete and not the abstract, with things which can be 'seen', either in real life or in pictures. In the primary school, for instance, children enjoy learning about sacred places - church, synagogue, mosque, etc. - and festivals. In the secondary school they can move on to such topics as pilgrimages, sacred writings, rites of passage, founders of religions and worship. It is not until pupils are fourteen or fifteen that they can really benefit from studying a religion as a whole, in contrast to the thematic study of the various aspects of religion which is appropriate in the earlier stages.

One of the aims of this kind of religious education is to help pupils to 'stand in other people's shoes', to discover what a religion looks - and feels - like to its adherents. And learning to stand in other people's shoes is an important element in moral education.

An emphatic study of religions, with its corollary of learning to accept and respect differences, makes an important contribution to pupils' understanding of the society in which they are growing up. This is as relevant for children in remote rural areas as it is for those who have frequent contact with members of ethnic minorities, because few people will remain in the same place for the whole of their lives. The children who are starting school now will spend their adult lives as citizens of the twenty-first century, and we are educating for the world that lies ahead, not for the world that lies behind us or even for the world that happens to exist at the moment in the more isolated parts of the country.

In recent years it has been suggested that religious education should include evaluation of religions, including evaluation of truth claims. The development of evaluative skills is certainly an important part of a pupil's education, but a profound knowledge of a religion is an absolute prerequisite for evaluating it and particularly its claims to truth, and the amount of knowledge which even bright sixth formers might have gained could lead only to the making of uninformed and simplistic judgements. To encourage pupils to evaluate religions is incompatible with helping them to stand in other people's shoes.

Learning about the different aspects of religion is one part of the study of the phenomena of religions. Another part is learning to understand the relationship between belief and life. This is not in any sense an attempt to ground morality in religion, but rather to illustrate the fact that one's ethical principles stem from one's beliefs about the nature of man and the nature of ultimate reality, whether those beliefs are religious or non-religious.

The relationship between belief and life was an element in the problem-centred discussion of the RE of the sixties. However, when religious education is understood as the study of religion the discussion of ethical issues needs to be undertaken in a completely different way, involving the reversal of the earlier order, which was discussion of a personal or social issue leading on to reference to religious teachings. But not only does the order need to be reversed; the task has to be tackled in two stages. First, a particular belief in a religion has to be unpacked, to discover, for example, what Christians mean by the doctrine of creation, or what they believe about the nature of man (acknowledging of course that there is never only one way in which a belief is interpreted within a religion). Then, and only then, can the next step be taken: discovering what the implications of the belief are for Christian attitudes and actions in relation to particular personal or social issues. This makes a clear distinction between those who hold the belief - the adherents of the religion - and the members of 4B, most of whom are unlikely to want to describe themselves as religious. The belief and its implications have authority for the former but not for the latter. When this distinction is made clear to a class they are freed to study the topic seriously without feeling that they are being got at.

The reaction of many secondary teachers may well be that their fourth and fifth forms would not be in the least attracted to the idea of unpacking the beliefs of any religion, apart from beliefs about life after death. However, it must be emphasised that this type of study becomes possible and interesting only when pupils' earlier experiences of religious education has been of an objective study of the phenomena of religions, structured in such a way that their understanding has been gradually and logically built up.

The relationship between belief and life may be tackled in a self-contained scheme of work, focusing as suggested above on selected beliefs of one or two religions. Or it may be included in a study of ultimate questions, that is, those questions which man asks about the meaning of his existence and to which there are no provable answers - questions such as What is man? Who am I? Who is my neighbour (especially in a conflict of interest situation)? Is there any meaning in life? Is death the end? How do I come to terms with evil and suffering? This can be a fascinating study for pupils in the upper part of the secondary school, doing, for instance, 'What is man?' at fourteen and 'Suffering' at fifteen or sixteen. The pupils first explore the questions raised by the topic and then look at the answers offered by some of the major religions and non-religious systems of beliefs, particularly those represented in this country.

As with the previous scheme, however, it is impossible to embark on this kind of study with fourteen- or fifteen-year-olds unless they have already built up some knowledge of the religions involved. Pupils are not able to make sense of the beliefs of a religion if they do not know how to handle its scriptures, its imagery, its symbolism, etc., and if they do not understand the characteristic uses of language in religion. Resources are a problem here. Most of the books produced by the educational publishers are of little use because they deal with the beliefs and practices of religions in such a brief and simplistic way that pupils have no possibility of getting anywhere near an understanding of what they mean in the life of the adherents of the religions. Books and other resources produced by the religions themselves, especially those prepared for their own children, are much more valuable, but while there are plenty for Judaism and an increasing number of Islam there are very few for Hinduism and Sikhism, and there is almost nothing on Christianity which matches the kind of material available on Judaism.

One other way in which pupils can be helped to understand the relationship between belief and life is through the use of biographies. However, these need to be very carefully selected. Humanists have been justified in their complaint that Christians appeared to be claiming a monopoly of such virtues as compassion, dedication and self-sacrifice, by using them as examples of Christianity in practice. There is justification, though, for studying the life and work of people who have been consciously and explicitly motivated by their beliefs, whatever religion or non-religious system they have been committed to. This use of biographies is really appropriate only in the secondary school. (See below, in the section on the exploration of experiences, for discussion of a different kind of biography which can also be used in the primary school.) Many Agreed Syllabuses, even recent ones, suggest using in the lower secondary school or even in the primary school the stories of people whose achievements cannot be adequately grasped by children of that age. In order to appreciate Martin Luther King's work, for example, it is necessary to understand the historical background of the slave trade and the complexities of race relations in the United States of America, and it would be wrong even to attempt to deal with these topics with younger pupils.

The second area I want to deal with is the **skills required for the study of religion.** These skills are not peculiar to religious education; they are required in a number of areas of the curriculum. What is distinctive is the particular cluster of them which pupils need to master if they are to understand the nature of religion. I shall select here only those which have some relevance to the ethical dimension of the curriculum.

The first is the ability to handle historical material, in order to learn not only what happened in the past but what criteria are appropriate for trying to discover what happened, and what weight different kinds of evidence can carry. Religions have histories, religions change and develop. A knowledge of the relevant periods of history and the criteria for studying the past is therefore essential for understanding religions. And this is a skill which is also needed by a morally educated person. We must all be aware of the way in which the lack of any historical dimension has rendered many discussions of ethical issues unbalanced and has led to the making of ill-informed judgements (like the claim of a well-known campaigner that the moral decline in Britain stemmed from the publication of John Robinson's Honest to God). The second skill is the ability to recognise distinctive uses of language. Language is used in a number of different ways in religion, particularly in worship and in credal statements, and many discussions about religion - and about moral questions - have been vitiated by the assumption that there is only one kind of language, that of the empirical sciences, and by the inability to recognise the logical status of different kinds of statements. Everything that is being done in the primary school to help children to become competent and confident in their handling of language and to understand the different ways in which words are used is making an important contribution to both religious education and moral education. Specific schemes of work are more appropriate in the upper secondary school. For example, fourteen or fifteen year olds could tackle 'What is belief?', asking what significance there is in the different ways in which we use the words belief and believe: 'I believe that there is a bus at 5.30 p.m.', 'I believe that he will never let me down', 'I believe that there is a God', 'I believe in God the Father', etc.

A valuable scheme of work for sixth formers, perhaps in the general studies course, could be 'Communication', including the ways in which language is used in different discourses of meaning.

The third skill is the ability to understand the use of symbolism, both in its verbal and non-verbal forms. Symbols play an important part in religion. They point to deeper and more profound meanings. When they are interpreted literally and their real meaning for the adherents of a religion is not recognised, it becomes virtually impossible to achieve the aim of standing in another person's shoes. For example, if pupils see a picture or image of Ganesha, the elephant-headed God of Hinduism, and do not know that the elephant symbolises wisdom and learning in Indian culture they are likely to come to the disparaging conclusion: 'Fancy worshipping a God who's got an elephant head!'

The fourth skill is the ability to distinguish the different kinds of question which man asks, the methods he uses to find answers to these questions, and the status of the answers reached. This skill is closely related to the ability to distinguish different uses of language. It is one which pupils should be gradually acquiring, not least through learning to identify the distinctive elements in topic work or other integrated courses, but at about thirteen or fourteen they could tackle directly a scheme of work on 'Asking questions'. This would begin by considering different kinds of empirical questions (e.g. How long is the playing field? How is a circuit board made? What effect does tobacco companies' sponsorship of sport have on young people's smoking?). Then one would move on to aesthetic questions (e.g. How does a composer – or artist or poet – achieve a particular effect? What is good music – or art or poetry?). Next, ethical questions (e.g. What do we mean when we call some actions 'good' and some 'bad'? Why are some actions considered right in one society and wrong in another, right in one period and wrong in another? How does one decide what is the right thing to do when one has to choose between two 'good' actions or two 'bad' actions?). Finally, ultimate questions (e.g. Is there life after death? Why are the answers to ultimate questions, whether given by theists or atheists, always in the form of beliefs?). This kind of study helps pupils to think more clearly – a valuable skill when discussing both religious and moral issues – and in addition one section of it enables them to focus in some detail on questions which deal with the nature of moral judgements and the factors affecting them.

Finally, I come to the third area of religious education: the exploration of experience. This was one of the main ingredients of the experience-based RE of the sixties, in which the pupils' experience was used as a starting point for the development of religious concepts. A different approach is required when the subject is understood as an objective study of religion, and when the development of religious concepts is seen as the task of the religious family and the religious community, and not as the task of the school. In this context experience can be interpreted as human experience in its widest sense, though with the youngest children it will obviously be right to focus mainly on their own experience.

Religions are concerned with man's experience. They offer, as do non-religious systems of belief, answers to the ultimate questions which man asks about the meaning of his existence. I suggested above that in the upper part of the secondary school it would be appropriate to undertake a serious study of one or more of these ultimate questions and of the answers offered by some of the religions and non-religious systems of belief. However, in the earlier years of schooling pupils can be encouraged to explore and reflect on those aspects of human experience which raise ultimate questions. This is particularly important in the primary school, and for the youngest children religious education should consist almost entirely of this exploration of experience, with learning about the phenomena of religions being mainly incidental.

Human experience themes are one of the ways in which the exploration of experience can be tackled. 'Human experience themes' is not a very happy expression, but I use it to distinguish them from the 'life themes' of the sixties, which tended to be general primary school topics with Bible stories added and which had a confessional aim. Life themes tended to be placed in religious education syllabuses in a haphazard order, so that, e.g. 'Homes and families' or 'Journeys' might be used with any age group from five to thirteen, but the sequence of themes is important, with both the children's stage of development and a particular ultimate question being taken into account. For instance, if a scheme on 'What is man?' is to be tackled at all adequately with thirteen- or fourteen-year-olds, with a direct study of the answers offered by religions and non-religious systems of belief, then it must be preceded by an exploration of and reflection on what it is to be a human being, and a human being in a community with other human beings. A possible sequence of themes would be 'Babies' and 'Homes and families' with the five to seven age group, 'Growing up' with the sevens to nines, and 'Who am I?' with the nines to elevens.

'Who is my neighbour?' is an ideal question for consideration in the junior school. Traditionally we have answered the question by telling the story of the Good Samaritan but, quite apart from the fact that the parable is really about the widening of the concept of neighbour from one's 'kith and kin', the answer to the question 'Who is my neighbour?' is obvious in that situation. It may not be easy to follow the Samaritan's example, but it is certainly easy to see what the right action was. Most of the decisions we have to take, however, are not as clearcut as that. How do we come to a decision when the legitimate interests of two individuals or two groups of people are in conflict? Children can be helped to be aware of conflict of interest when they undertake a study of their own village or neighbourhood. For example, whose interest should be given priority when there is a proposal to build houses on a recreation ground, or to take some of a farmer's land for a by-pass? Some years ago an excellent series of books was produced for use in the junior school, which encouraged this awareness of the complexity of many of the decisions which communities have to make. The series dealt with What Happens When . . . An Airport is Enlarged, A Village

Grows, A Valley is Drowned, etc.[5].

Possible human experience themes in the secondary school are: 'Barriers', 'Survival', 'Fear', 'Conflict', 'Freedom'. Unlike the earlier life themes, there may be no explicit mention of religion in human experience themes. If a religious example or story is appropriate then of course it doesn't need to be excluded just because it is religious, but religious material has to be judged by exactly the same criteria as any other material: is it the best possible vehicle for helping pupils to explore a particular aspect of human experience? The aim is to raise questions, not to moralise, and not to offer the 'right' answer, and certainly not to offer a particular religious answer, because by definition ultimate questions are questions to which there is no univerally agreed answer.

Biographies can also be used for the exploration of experience. I referred above to the use of carefully selected biographies to illustrate the relationship between belief and action. For this different purpose one would choose the biographies of people whose lives give greater insight into particular human qualities, irrespective of their religious or other commitment. Biographies can present situations in personal and concrete terms so that pupils can discuss them realistically in a way which is impossible when they are presented with an issue in a vacuum. So many of the 'moral dilemmas' produced for use in secondary schools are unsatisfactory in this respect. Before one could say what one would do in a particular situation one would need a great deal more information than is given in a quarter-page description. A good biography (and I don't mean the little outline summaries of a person's life which one sometimes meets) can provide sufficient background information to enable pupils to imagine themselves into the situation.

Fiction is probably one of the best ways of encouraging

children to explore and reflect on human experience. There is a wealth of excellent children's literature available for every age group. As with biographies, it is easier for pupils to stand in other people's shoes if they know enough about the characters to be able to identify with them, to understand the pressures on them which have made them act or react in a particular way, to recognise that motives are often mixed, and to realise that intentions and actions are not always identical.

It could be argued that in one sense there is nothing which does not involve some exploration of human experience. However, it is those aspects of human experience which raise ultimate questions that are most relevant to religious education, and, I would suggest, to moral education. To discover whether what we are doing is making that kind of contribution we need to ask: Does it help the pupils to understand themselves, other people and the natural world better? Does it help them to understand better their relationship with other people and with the natural world? And does it raise questions for them about man's experience and about the mystery of what it is to be human?

I have described three areas in religious education – the study of the phenomena of religions, the mastery of the kind of skills needed for the study of religion, and the exploration of experience. I believe that these can make a significant contribution to the ethical dimension of the curriculum. I have not dealt with what has frequently been understood as moral education, and equally frequently regarded as the responsibility of religious education: telling children 'moral' stories and giving them 'moral' teaching, partly because I see the aim of religious education in quite different terms – as helping pupils to understand the nature of religion – and partly because I am convinced that this is in any case a completely ineffectual way of 'making children moral'. Nor have I dealt with those most important ingredients of moral

education: the ethos of the school, the atmosphere in the classroom, and the example of the staff, because this is a shared
responsibility, with the pupils' experience in maths or art or
physical education lessons being just as crucial for their moral
development as their experience in religious education.

Notes

1 Loukes, H., Teenage Religion, SCM Press, 1961.

2 Loukes, H., New Ground in Christian Education, SCM Press, 1965.

3 Crowther Report, 1959, Vol. 1, p. 44.

4 For a fuller treatment, see Holm, J., Teaching Religion in School, Oxford University Press, 1975.

5 Bell, G., Oliver and Boyd, 1970.

Chapter 11

SCHOOL ASSEMBLIES AND THE BOUNDARIES OF MORAL EDUCATION

Brian Gates

The setting is the large hall of a primary school[1]. Over a hundred children, their teachers, and a handful of parents are gathered for the Friday mid-morning assembly.

The teacher who is leading the assembly invites the infants to guess what the assembly is about from the mimes of the older children during the first HYMN.

MIME: 2 children enter, sit at table, eat, get up, wash at chair (sink), and clean teeth.

Infants successfully interpret the actions in their own words.

The teacher then announces that the assembly is on the theme of teeth and a board is turned round to reveal some children's paintings.

Several children in succession come to the front and read various pieces of information, which they have written out, on teeth.

Other children file through the hall carrying large cardboard teeth, corresponding with the particular type mentioned by the (child) narrator: together they form the plan of a mouthfull of teeth.

The narrator points to a diagram of a tooth pinned to the blackboard and another child describes it.

Lower junior children then file to the front holding pictures of food; they sit in front of the teeth while the song 'Food, glorious food' is playing.

Another child appears, sits in front of the others, and recites the poem 'I wish I'd looked after my teeth ...'.

He is then inspected by the girl dentist;   she checks each of his teeth in turn.

The group of children who had previously read out information on teeth now return with further information, this time about how teeth decay, what to eat and what not to eat.

The dentist explains how to brush teeth and how often to go for a check up.

The teacher then invites everyone to PRAY
-   giving thanks for dentists and toothpaste
-   asking to be reminded to clean teeth
-   asking to be reminded to eat properly
-   giving thanks for teeth
-   thinking about the school and all who spend their days in it.

A child reads his own account of his last trip to the dentist.

All join in singing a second HYMN: 'I love the sun', including a verse about God making our teeth.

The teacher explains that her class have also been doing maths on the topic of teeth.

Two children appear with charts: one is a bar graphshowing which is the most popular tooth-paste in the class;   the other shows how many points (two a day for two weeks) each child in the class has earned for cleaning teeth.

Children with maximum points are invited to the front and applauded by the other children.

Final message from teacher: visit your dentist;   watch what you eat; take your toothpaste and brush on holiday with you!

Such an assembly as this can be found in any day of the week in schools throughout England and Wales.   Not least because of seating constraints, the secondary variant might involve only a section of the school at any one time. Yet in one shape or another, an assembly regularly takes place in the majority of schools, with a similar mixture of ingredients[2].

Reaction from an outsider will be predictably varied. An immediately critical judgement might begin by commenting that the presentation is too orchestrated and lacking in spontaneity, the tone is moralistic, and worst of all, there is confusion between belief in God and the need for dental hygiene. More positively, it might be remarked that here there is demonstrably a 'prizing of persons'. The children are involved in an occasion which encourages them to express themselves in public; care has been taken in the preparation and this is reflected in the stimuli and modes of expression that are used; and the whole experience is earthed in the children's own experience. Moreover, the clarity and warmth which are high priorities in any inter-personal morality of communication are much in evidence.

Judgements like these abound within the teaching profession, reflecting a genuine ambivalence as to the worth of assemblies. Their persistence, however, is hardly surprising in view of the tradition behind them[3]. They were legally underwritten by the 1944 Education Act, but ante-date the establishment of Board School Education in 1870. Records suggest that, if anything, they have become the more elaborate over the years[4]. The DES for its part has loosened the legal tightness of 'all together every day', while encouraging schools to maintain this communal expression of their ethos[5]. Thus, school assemblies, religious education and moral education are part of some peculiar English and Welsh mix.

Yet that very mix can be painfully embarrassing. The telling portraits in If and Kes are matched in a wide range of educationist opinion from the last decade or so, culminating in John Hull's School Worship: an Obituary[6]. Where some have been content to campaign for abolition, others have demanded as a preliminary the clarification of intent (aims and objectives), and warned against category confusion: What is an assembly?   What is worship? Anyway, it is worth rehearsing the views that are forthcoming from the different educational disciplines. Somewhat artificially, they can be represented as follows:

Sociologist:

'1 Don't be misled by appearances. Watch out for the **latent** as well as the **manifest** functions of assemblies in school. In particular, notice how the occasion can be used to underwrite the authority and position of the head-teacher. One can learn a great deal about the character and structure of a particular school from the way the assemblies are organised.

2 No community known to humankind has been without its rites and rituals, its moments of anniversary, memorial and celebra- tion – family birthday parties, weddings and funerals; the national equivalents; May Day parades, religious festivals. These are marks of the identity of that community. Where they wither and decay, so too the community itself may be withering, or at least undergoing major change. In that a school strives to be a community it is invariably involved in ritual actions. The problem then is to distinguish between ritual which authentically declares the special identity of this particular group of teachers and pupils, and ritual which is little more than an empty shell taken over second-hand.'

Psychologist:

'1 Don't be misled by appearances. When children go through the motions of an assembly, they may well be missing as persons. Concentration span is limited, especially when a read- ing is long and droning, and the floor uncomfortable. The range of individual levels of understanding at an assembly is enormous; how is it possible to reach them all?

2 Don't underestimate the importance of a sense of belonging in the process of individual becoming. Some opportunity for a boy or girl to see themselves in relation to both older and younger children – whether idolising, fearing, imitating or caring – is as fundamental as the experience of being mothered and fathered.'

Philosopher:

'1 Don't be misled by appearances. An assembly to deal with notices and matters of school organisation is one thing, an Act of Worship is quite another. There is no justification for this in a county-maintained school, law or no law. If it is compulsory, then it is immoral and offensive to individual conscience. If voluntary, then it is divisive. Either way, it is out of place in state schools.

2 But an assembly of part or the whole school can be of great educational value. If, that is, it takes seriously the differences of belief and unbelief found within the school, and then goes on to explore the different values associated with them. Throughout the curriculum, throughout the individual lives of teachers and pupils, there are presuppositions, loyalties, commitments, customs, doubts - all worth exploring, whether in the form of individual teacher, pupil, class, or subject presentation. The assembly then becomes an occasion for focussing attention on the issues and values at the heart of the school as community - for exploring them, bemoaning or celebrating them.'

Theologian:
'1 Don't be misled by appearances. An act of genuine worship is not fairly represented by a hymn-prayer sandwich. This is as distant from the real thing as it is from the multi-media mediaeval Christian liturgy, or the rhythm of an African tribal festival. Religious communities are increasingly more aware of this in their own lives and can reflect it in their own educational provisions.

2 It is theologically blasphemous, in any setting, to suppose that one can **compel** a person to worship. In a mixed society, it is hard to find theological justification for regular acts of Christian worship in secular schools. At the same time, school assemblies without either hymns or prayers can still be complementary to a spirit of worship, especially if they provide encouragement for dwelling on matters of substance in the life of the school.

3 Such alternative assemblies might well on occasion involve stories, music, drama, dance drawn from particular religious traditions. From time to time, there might be demonstrations by groups of believers from within the school of their own modes of worship; even on occasion attempts at some deliberately inter-faith presentation. For without some opportunity to put themselves in the shoes of those who would worship, any child is probably missing out on forms of understanding and experience that s/he might find both personally enriching and theologically challenging.

Quite how typical are the views sketched here as from the different disciplines, is open to debate. It certainly is currently orthodoxy[7] that the formal act of worship in school lacks the proper educational grounds now widely credited to both religious and moral education[8]. Although any orthodoxy deserves to be questioned, in this case it also deserves to be more widely canvassed for staff-room discussion, and with it the kinds of positive alternatives which have also been mentioned.

With that prospect in mind, what might now be said about the significance of assemblies for moral education? It may help to maintain the convention of different educational perspectives and to list their questions and comments in turn.

From both philosopher and theologian we hear: 'Is the school making a proper distinction between secular assemblies and acts of worship? There is much that can be contributed to moral education from secular assemblies, for instance in the priority that is given to sharing - of ideas, interests, activities found in the life of the school - a message is articulated that would also imply a moral argument for curriculum integration[9]. Making connections, recognising achievements, celebrating worth deserve priority also in relation to the world beyond the school. Assemblies can provide the occasion for extending horizons into local, regional, national and international realms, whether with a visit from the 'lollipop lady' and local vet, or with some mock election, an international festival and a North-South tribunal.

Any of these examples could be set within the context of an explicit act of Christian (or other) worship, but such setting can easily be immoral in its insensitivity to diversity of starting points. On the other hand, it can also be a quite proper expression of the faith on which the school itself was founded; but, even in a church school, it will be more appropriate in some than others to assume confessional allegiance on the part of all the pupils[10].

Certainly there is a need to give recognition to minorities, including religious minorities, within the school[11]. An assembly can do this, and there are rich resources for doing so in many areas of the country;though some sharing in an act of worship need not be ruled out here, more often the multi-cultural and multi-faith assembly will be designed primarily to be informing.

By the psychologist we are asked what care is taken to check intelligibility in our assemblies. Visiting speakers are at a special disadvantage when faced with wide age and ability spread and poor acoustics. Research has indicated that on the whole readings make little impact and tend not to be remembered[12]; the Welsh Office has gone so far as to suggest that the didactic approach is generally counter-productive[13]. Clearly, there are other modes of learning that can equally be deployed for an assembly.

The fact that imitation is a powerful source for moral and immoral learning suggests that special attention be given to the modelling that goes on in an assembly. Who leads? Who is mentioned? What stories are chosen and how exclusive are the heroes and anti-heroes contained in them?[14] The impact of an assembly in terms of moral education can no doubt be increased with the benefit of a wide repertoire of well chosen stories, images and bodily gestures!

In turn, the sociologist presses for a policy in the school about how the assemblies are organised, by whom and to what end? Has this been talked through, as might a reading scheme or exam provision, for the whole school? How often are staff meetings devoted to the matter of assemblies?

He also asks how much participation there is. If the answer is 'little', is this not opportunity missed? If 'much', how is 'vying' between individuals and classes avoided? Are the children who are called on to present an assembly theme ever allowed to become a 'front' behind which I, as teacher, can hide? Finally, are there any means of exploring or expressing the sense of identity within a school as a community that are unduly neglected? Playing games in an assembly could prove to be a high order moral activity!

With or without the benefit of academic disciplines, it is evident that there are many different sorts of school assembly. They can be arranged for clarity's sake on a simple continuum, as follows:

N O S S E M B L Y	administrative occasion for sharing information about school routine	informing **about** e.g.: a subject, event, work of another, or festival	sharing **in** e.g.: a subject, event, work of another so it comes alive: debating, exploring, expressing	W O R S H I P

This arrangement corresponds to that employed by the Writing Research Unit at London Institute of Education[15], and widely used since. Their same poles of functional and expressive/poetic as applied to varieties of children's written work in school are here redeployed to interpret assemblies. Degrees of personal involvement increase towards the right-hand pole, but this is not to deny the importance also of what is on the left. Each sort of assembly is capable of becoming formality, and in all value-assumptions are implicit - more or less routinised - and judgements have been made about what matters. On the right, the values are usually more explicit, yet even here there is risk that they can still be treated in a closed way. Just as it has been important to establish that religious and moral education in schools are continuous in their enquiring methods with the rest of the curriculum, so too with assemblies, if their grounds for survival are not to beg too many questions.

At this point, the main argument of this chapter needs to be more plainly asserted. It has been suggested that assemblies are significant in a variety of possible ways for moral education. Where they do not occur an opportunity for initiative and experiment with a large community is missed, and in turn, boys and girls may have less discriminating sense to bring to their working involvement in mass meetings or leisured excitement in football crowds. In all this the aspects of moral education which have been most frequently referred to have been mainly related to interpersonal relationships, sensitivity to the views of others, social justice, community action and aesthetic delight. Equally important for moral education are questions about the worthwhileness of any action or conviction - why at the end of the day they are worth bothering about. It is here, at the level of motivation and intention, that the deepest concerns of religious and moral education overlap. It is here too that the authentic act of worship and the short play, the singing, the personal statement of political conviction, etc. trade in the realm of comparable assumptions.

A fully-fledged act of Christian worship pre-supposes a theological focus, in effect, a belief in God. Few schools cannot take this belief for granted (could they ever?) for all their pupils and staff; but **all** have, in a sense, a hole in their foundations, into which from time to time teachers and pupils alike may stare. This image is partly prompted by the comment of the eight-year-old that 'a floor is so you won't fall through the hole your house stands on', and also by N.F. Simpson's play The Hole in which a group clusters round a hole in the road and muses over the goings-on within.

The theatre critic Martin Esslin once remarked that the Theatre of the Absurd is something of a contemporary religious quest; for it expresses a tragic sense of loss of ultimate certainties and strives to make man aware of the ultimate realities of his condition, to instil in him again the lost sense of cosmic wonder and primeval anguish, to shock him out of an existence that has become trite, mechanical, complacent, and deprived of the dignity that comes of awareness. For God is dead, above all, to the masses who live from day to day and have lost all contact with the basic facts – and mysteries – of the human condition with which, in former times, they were kept in touch through the living ritual of their religion, which made them parts of a real community and not just atoms in an atomised society. (16)

In similar vein the suggestion is now advanced that assemblies operate in this field. They can provide opportunity for exploring basic beliefs, loyalties and commitments; those of teachers, pupils or parents; national, international and domestic; and of specific groups. In so far as they do this, they will reveal a pre-occupation with the same boundary questions of human being that no moral education that retains its salt can afford to ignore. In other words, an act of worship, a school assembly, a moral response have all at core much to do with each other.

To conclude: There is real advantage that comes from our mixed constitutional heritage. We do not have in England and Wales an impenetrable barrier between religion and the stage; that American arrangement has made it difficult for critical discussion of basic beliefs to be entertained in school. Nor do we have, for the most part at least, an exclusive induction into one particular ideological framework; that Soviet programme does not encourage openness in interpretation either. Rather we have confirmed by the 1944 Education Act a mixture of secular state with parental religious community. The intervening years have seen the breadth of Christian denominationalism which was recognised there, widened in many Local Education Authorities to include other religious traditions and secular humanism[17]. There are important ramifications here for religious education, for school assemblies, for moral education and the whole curriculum. Beware of the boundaries!

Notes

1 This account is based upon an assembly in a primary school in North West England in 1981 and the author expresses his gratitude to the school concerned.

2 Surveys which have investigated the frequency, timing, length, order and key ingredients of assemblies are available. See Jones, C.M., Worship in the Secondary School, Religious Education Press, 1969; Schools Council, Working Paper 44: R.E. In Primary Schools, Longman, 1972; County Survey of R.E., West Glamorgan, 1979; Gates, B.E., How They Assemble: a report on the act of worship in Lancashire Schools, S. Martin's College, 1982. Also, the current work of P. Souper of the Education Department, Southampton University, on the conduct of assemblies regionally and nationally.

3 Hull, J.M., 'Worship in the County School 1870-1965', in his Worship - an Obituary, SCM Press, 1975; also, Jones, C.M. op.cit.

4 This is reflected in the increasingly elaborate statement about the Act of Worship found in LEA Agreed Syllabuses; See Williams, J.G., Worship and the Modern Child, SPCK, 1957, commonly quoted in subsequent syllabuses. The irony of RE and school assemblies becoming more elaborate when society itself was if anything, becoming less overtly involved with church-going is made much of in Cannon, C., 'Influence of Religion on Education Policy, 1902-44', British Journal of Education Studies, Vol. 12, no. 2, 1964.

5 See, DES Reports on Education 58, September 1969.

6 Despite several attempts to discredit John Hull personally after the publication of this book, he was already establised as a respected teacher and writer in the field of RE; he is the editor of the British Journal of Religious Education (then called Learnir for Living) and Senior Lecturer in Educational Studies at Birmingham University.

7 See Dearden, R.F. Philosophy of Primary Education, Routledge and Kegan Paul, 1968; Schools Council, Working Paper 44: RE in Primary Schools, Evans Methuen, 1972; Cole, W.O., 'School Worship - a Reconsideration, Learning for Living', Vol. 13, no. 2, 1974; Webster, D., 'School Worship - The Way Ahead?', Learning for Living, Vol. 14, no. 2, 1974; ILEA, Assemblies in County Schools, 1978; The Durham Report: The Fourth R, SPCK, 1970 presents the argument for continuing

the act of worship for all pupils, by analogy with the attendance of a 'mixed' congregation on civic occasions. The particular weakness of this comparison is the degree of 'voluntariness' involved in the school occasion. See the comment of Edwin Cox and Ninian Smart in Learning for Living, Vol. 10, no. 1, 1970.

8   The problem of arriving at a curriculum rationale for moral education has seemed in principle to be less difficult than for RE. Thus Hirst, P., 'Morals and Religions in the Maintained School', British Journal of Educational Studies, Vol. 14, no. 1, 1965, is confident that public norms for agreeing what constitutes morality are easily available. This stance and that of Peters, R.S., Ethics and Education, Routledge and Kegan Paul, 1960, has been largely shared by John Wilson, Richard Pring and others. Peter McPhail too, while less conceptual in emphasis, is confident that ME justifies itself in terms of the concerns which arise from inter-personal encounter - almost a social-psychology version of natural law.

For RE the need for critical justification has entailed demonstrating that its grounds in the curriculum do not depend primarily on legal requirement or ecclesiastical tradition, but on the nature of religion as a form of knowledge and the continuing interest of boys and girls in the fundamental questions and insights which, together, constitute the religious experience of mankind past and present. The work of Ninian Smart has been especially important in this field, for example Secular Education and the Logic of Religion, Faber, 1968.

A summary of some of the debate in curriculum philosophy is found in Gates, B.E., 'RE: a proper humanism', London Educational Review, Vol. 2, no. 3, 1973. The Schools Council Groundplan for the Study of Religion, 1977, provides a theoretical taxonomy for the subject and Discovering an Approach, Macmillan, 1977, sets out the potential for Primary R.E. Arguably, the lack of consensus in society generally on moral questions and the common roots of religion and morality in the heart of personal intention, belief and belonging bring the matter of the mutuality of RE and ME back into focus.

9   This is implicit in much of James, C., Young Lives at Stake, Collins, 1968, and apparent in the more recent vogue in references to "Moral Education Across the Curriculum".

10 For instance, the Roman Catholic Voluntary Aided Church School is more deliberately concerned to introduce boys and

girls to the full practice and beliefs of the parent community of faith than the equivalent Anglican school which is seen as contributing to **national** educational provision. The distinction is set out in The Fourth R (op.cit.). In addition, the local catchment of a church school may well bring in children of other than believing Christian backgrounds. How the school treats this minority/majority is critical both morally and theologic

11 The issues here are the very theological ones which are the present preoccupation of both the World Council of Churches and the Vatican in their substantial dialogue with other faiths. Responses as to what is appropriate in schools in England and Wales can be found in National Catholic Commission for Racial Justice Where Creed and Colour Matter: A Survey of Black Children in Catholic Schools, Catholic Information Office, 1975 and Church School Education and Islam in Multi-faith Manchester, Manchester CE Diocesan Council for Education, 1981.

12 See McPhail, P., op.cit., Appendix A.

13 Welsh Office Education Survey, No. 3, Religious Education in the Secondary Schools of Wales, HMSO, 1975.

14 The lack of stories from beyond white and Western Europe is at last being recognised in more recent content selections for anthologies for assemblies. See, Hedges, S., With One Voice, Religious Education Press, 1970; Butler, D.G., Many Lights, Geoffrey Chapman, 1975; Purton, R., Festivals and Celebration, Blackwell, 1981.

15 Martin, N., et al., Writing and Learning Across the Curriculum 11-16, Ward Lock, 1976; also, Britton, J., 'What's the use? A schematic account of language function', Educational Review, vol. 23, no. 1, 1970.

16 Esslin, M., The Theatre of the Absurd, Penguin, 1968.

17 See, for instance, Avon, Birmingham and ILEA.

Chapter 12

PROGRAMMES AND MATERIALS IN MORAL EDUCATION

Gerald H. Gardiner

Scene:-   Class of fifteen-year-olds - in progress for ten min-
             utes. The door opens and a boy casually walks to his
             seat.

TEACHER: Excuse me! .... You had something to say?

BOY: No! - Don't think so.

TEACHER: Like - Sorry I'm late but ....

BOY: Why? - Yea I'm late but I ain't sorry! Do you
             want me to lie?

This is a trivial incident, with very little moral quality about
it, and easily, perhaps rightly, ignored in the routine of a busy
teacher. But it does illustrate that the path of the moral educator is set about with disturbing, odd, and often personal questions. Can anyone expect to offer pupils a moral education if he
is not himself morally educated?

Any teacher considering ME would be well advised to read and
reflect on as much philosophy, theology, sociology and psychology
as he can 'enjoy'[1]. Although the aim of this chapter is to consider programmes and materials, the starting place must be
outside the classroom. Teachers must at least know what they
are attempting to do. They should explore the morality of the
assumptions made by the various schemes and approaches, otherwise they can be caught up in practice with a system that on
deeper examination they might not really wish to defend. They
could be setting for themselves and their students aims and

objectives that at their best are unrealistic, and at their worst could be described as threatening. The teacher of ME should be realistically informed about the size and implications of the task, and to acknowledge the limitations of their venture.

This is not to say that the average teacher has to be a philosopher – king, or a saint, but the qualification is essential to the extent of being able to give a reasoned account of the place and function of ME, first of all to himself, and then to wider audiences under the banner of accountability. Hopefully the adolescent students will put the question 'Why Moral Education?' And they are the most difficult audience to satisfy.

It is necessary that the school should see any involvement in moral education in perspective and context. So much development has happened, and continues to happen long before and long after school. The family has played a foundational part before the school pupil was able to say 'moral values', let alone grasp their significance. Religious categories and authorities need not be quite as dead as the sixties theologians would have us believe; the influence lingers in many guises. The peer group and the 'pop' world of fashion and music exert pressures. The organisation of the school and the hidden curriculum can both enable and hinder ME; the attitudes of staff and a thousand other factors all intermesh. Each could be examined to see how it might affect moral education, and much has of course been written. In so many ways, there can be interaction in the classroom, tension, laughter, anger or aggression, or sheer mystification because one or more of these background factors impinge on a given scheme, and react with the material being used.

One of the assumptions behind this chapter is that classroom-based ME is possible and profitable, either through existing subjects, or under its own name. Some in the field of moral education would question this assumption, and prefer to work at the general ethos of the school, its aims and objectives, the parent/ teacher organisation, student democracy, etc., before using a programme of ME. John Wilson develops his ideas about social organisation and moral education in Part IV of his book Practical Methods of Moral Education, and the Kohlbergian approach has in the Custer School (or school within a school) the entire curriculum centred on moral considerations[2].

This chapter assumes no such commitment, and takes as its starting place a small team of teachers in a comprehensive school. Here it has been agreed through whatever policy-making processes the school uses, to have a programme of moral education for the fourth and fifth year students. They proceed on the basis that as moral development is happening before, during and after school, that the curriculum as a minimum and basic starting base, should have a scheme of moral education. Its purpose is twofold.

(a) to explain the nature of morality, its language and the area of experience covered by the term.

(b) to help create the conditions that will nurture the healthy development of moral education.

Whether it will be labelled ME, or whether it will be part of the existing R.E., 'Guidance' or some other common core, can be left open. What materials are available, what approaches can be deployed?

Lifeline – Schools Council Project in Moral Education
(For a detailed understanding of the project see 'Moral Education in the Secondary School' by Peter McPhail)[3].

This is by far the most detailed and developed programme easily available to schools this side of the Atlantic. It was first published in 1972 and was based on three surveys designed to find out from boys and girls in secondary schools what sort of treatment they expected others to give them, to discover what their behavioural reactions were to various forms of treatment which they labelled 'good' and 'bad' and to identify their problems over the behaviour and the treatment of others.

As such then the project does not have a philosophical or psychological base, though Lifeline might claim that its aim is to develop a rewarding life-style in which people take other's needs, interests and feelings into consideration, as well as their own; in short a 'considerate life-style'. It starts with 'the customer' or at least with the customer a decade ago. Peter McPhail is in the process of revamping and updating the project material. Until the new or revised materials appear, the Lifeline programme has three parts.

1. In other people's shoes.
2. Proving the rule.
3. What would you have done?

Along with these there is a handbook on the practice of democracy by secondary school pupils.

Essentially, the scheme progresses from simple towards complex situations. The first part is sub-divided into:-

Sensitivity,

Consequences,

Points of View.

These consist of a series of cards, each depicting a situation that could be called a moral dilemma, if the term can be stretched from would-be suicide to sniffing!

e.g. Picture of a person on a very high bridge looking down at the river below. This has the caption:-

You know that your best friend is doing something which is causing him or her to suffer.

Then comes the question used throughout the series of cards.

"What do you do?"

Another card has a sketch of two people sitting side by side at desks with the caption:-

The person in the next desk to you sniffs continually.
"What do you do?"

These discussion or role-play starters are based on the view that "to become morally educated it is necessary to become sensitive to others, to learn to think about what consequences one's actions may have, and further to be inclined to act upon the understanding which derives from increased moral awareness." They are concerned with familiar situations at home, school or in the local neighbourhood. A class could easily make their own sets of cards and this would be a useful exercise in updating material.

The **'Consequences'** approach, again a series of cards, asks the question: "What happens when ....?" and gives students practice in working out the consequences of an action. The consequences situations are not limited to just two characters, and the belief behind them is that thinking in terms of consequences is basic to consideration for others.

'Points of View' is basically concerned with two people and asks directly how the other individual is affected. In this way a student would be invited to identify with another person. The Project team write, 'Reason, imagination and identification with others produce more considerate behaviour'. Then the question is made personal. **"What would you do?"**.

Proving the Rule comes as a series of five booklets, but instead of one or two people being involved, the series is concerned with personal and social identity relationships within groups, and conflict between different groups. They explore the 'rules' that might exist at a youth club, or a school, on the road for a motorcyclist, or in the home. Students are invited to ask themselves .... 'How would you feel about these rules if you were Paul?' (The boy in the story.) And 'Can you think of ways other than making rules which might improve the situation at home for everybody in the family?' Each situation ends with a series of questions to be considered, and exercises entitled 'Things to do'. These range from an invitation to "Draw or describe how you would like to look saying what advantages and what disadvantages if any it would have", to "Find out about the story of Narcissus."

Illustrations and fashions tend to date very quickly, as can be imagined, with references to Bob Dylan, Paul Simon or the film 'Easy Rider', being spot-on ten or twelve years ago, but needing considerable introduction in the 'eighties'. The final booklet in the series poses the question 'Why should I?', and considers the authority of adults, and slogans, of science, and myths, traditions and procedures. All booklets include a suggested reading and related materials list.

The third series puts the question, 'What would you have done?' through six booklets, each dealing with a real-life historical situation: South Africa, 1904, solitary confinement, 1917, Amsterdam, 1944, Los Angeles, 1965, Vietnam, 1966, and Gale, a drug addict in hospital, 1969. They are longer, more complex, and require a greater appreciation of the historical context, in order to really feel the moral dilemma being presented. The material can be used individually, but has been designed as a whole programme, and obvious benefit should come from being used in conjunction with each other. The handbook provides diagrams of the total scheme at work.

Overall, Lifeline presents the teacher with a flexible 'middle-of-the-road' approach to ME. There is the total scheme duly explained in the Schools Council publication, and yet there is room to use some or adapt some of the material and methods. "The teacher should not inhibit discovery by saying too much, too soon, too often", provides a sound warning, but at the same time "this is not equivalent to taking a permanent neutral stand."

The authors openly believe in their pattern of moral education, yet make no claim to be a universal authority in the field. The teacher of R.E. is invited to make use of techniques and materials, and if they think that their religious education is improved then "we are certainly not going to be resentful".

They offer a rule of thumb for testing approaches and materials in ME, which has an inviting pragmatic quality. "As long as we submit approaches to be used with children to discussion and trial, there is little fear if we believe that truth is self-authenticating. Teachers sensitive to the responses of their children and children's parents and their colleagues should not be fearful of trying what they judge to be potentially useful."[4] Quite so!!

The Farmington Trust – John Wilson Approach[5]

It is best to describe this response to ME in schools as 'an approach' because there is very little actually in print for classroom use in comparison to the Lifeline project. For the teacher who considers that skills in moral thinking are a priority, then the Wilson style should commend itself. "It is the method of acquainting the pupils, consciously and overtly, with morality as a subject or area of thought; making them aware of the skills, techniques and qualities required to get the right answers to moral questions".

'Right' at this stage of the moral quest means having followed the correct methodology of the subject, using the analysis set out below. John Wilson is as suspicious of a partisan method of ME as he is doubtful of the value of what he calls 'excessive vagueness, talk about sensitivity, maturity, caring etc.' He refers to these as 'unhelpfully global'.

If a teacher involved in a ME course has any interest in philosophy then this approach will have particular appeal. Wilson is, at base, a philosopher who argues for encouraging the use of reason in moral education, though not it must be added to the exclusion of emotion and imagination. He does not ignore the affective side, but he does want to direct ME towards the development of moral skills, rather than to imparting specific values.

He offers the following breakdown of components that put together cover the moral domain.

PHIL   the attitude which accepts others as equal.

EMP   the insight into the feelings of oneself (**AUTEMP**) and of others (**ALTEMP**).

GIG   the knowledge necessary for making rational moral judgements, especially an understanding of consequences.

DIK   the system of values which a person formulates and commits himself to.

PHRON   the system of values relating mainly to oneself.

KRAT   the ability to put moral principles into practice.

This method of considering ME naturally lends itself to classroom use. John Wilson in his book Practical Methods of Moral Education supports his approach because it is 'honest', 'professional' and perhaps above all as far as the average pupil is concerned, 'it gives the children something to hang onto.'[6]   This is often a neglected aspect of ME. Students may be invited to take part in all sorts of sensitive and imaginative excercises that have thoroughly convinced the teachers concerned as to their worth and purpose, but the youngsters are left without any sense of achievement. The 'something to hang onto' has therefore a special part to play, because it is not a creed or a faith, but rather a rational method for rational creatures, through which they can identify and solve moral problems. I wonder if it could be likened to the satisfaction in gaining the skill to sort out the puzzles presented by Rubik's Cube?

Teachers who prefer open-ended approaches, or methods that imply that there are no answers will not warm to the Wilson style. But he warns that this is the slippery path toward relativism. However it must be stressed that teaching the 'right' method does not imply the teaching of 'right answers', but a methodology for the pupil's own use: sometimes by direct didactic explaining of

the rules and the language, sometimes through controlled discussions, and often by using life situations, so that the essential range
of moral components can be understood and felt. Human emotion
is not ignored despite all the philosophical grounding of the
approach. In fact, John Wilson seems to see R.E. as coming into
its own at this point[7].

Some of the assumptions made about class discussion seem
rather remote from the average comprehensive school. The rules
suggested for governing wrong attitudes or wrong moves or style,
would be very difficult to implement unless the pupils concerned
were both intelligent and articulate. Yet throughout his programmes he maintains that his approach is both academic and
social, and resists strongly any separation of the two. Such a
union is healthy but difficult to achieve in a day school. Boarding
schools obviously offer more possibilities.

He puts his case in these terms. "We do not just put them
in a sailing ship and let life teach them; we discuss the experience while they are on the ship, take films and tape-recordings
of how they behave and consider what general principles emerge.
We do not just tell them to love their neighbours; we use examples, illustrations from books, films and real life; we get them to
role-play and act such illustrations for themselves."[8]

The method applied for example to a study of 'Old Age', would
need to include 'hard facts' about the problems of failing health
and advancing years; this would be **GIG**. To understand why a
perhaps feeble Grandpa is as important as another human being
PHIL would have to be discussed. To develop understanding of
how old people feel, **EMP** would have to emerge, and connected
with all this, to make decisions there would be **KRAT**. Holding
the exercise together, and pointing towards a wider system of
values, to which an individual could be committed would be **DIK**.
Analysed in this way on paper, the approach can seem to be formal

and artificial, but in practice there can emerge a creative dialogue between theory and practice, and a realistic balance between teacher authority and pupil exploration as the moral
components are taught, and felt, analysed and acted on. In my
opinion he achieves his aim of 'draining a little of the swamp to
give a practical educator a bit of firm ground to stand on'[9]. His
critics might suggest that his approach should really be described
as an 'O' level in moral philosophy!!

Values – Clarification

The twin names met time and time again under this approach
to ME are Sidney B. Simon and Louis E. Raths[10]. It could well
be described as a deceptively attractive method for classroom use
– attractive because the various 'strategies' are easy to set-up,
and often have a natural appeal to young people. They are at
times similar to a certain style of personality quiz often found
in teenage magazines. The deceptive quality is there because
at its heart, this method is very challenging to orthodox views of
morality.

The values-clarification approach in its philosophy considers
that the only 'democratic' route to psychological and ethical maturity is to free children to choose and create their own values.
In the past 'we' taught children – 'we' being parents and teachers
– that, for example, lying and cheating and stealing were wrong.
According to the V/C approach the encumbrances of adult 'no-
nos' have to be removed, and a specific seven-step value process
is prescribed. This is usually described as follows:-

CHOOSING:- (1) freely

(2) from alternatives

(3) after thoughtful consideration of the consequences of each alternative.

PRIZING:- (4) cherishing, being happy with the choice

(5) enough to be willing to confirm the choice
to others.

ACTING:-   (6)   or doing something with the choice

          (7)   repeatedly, in some pattern of life.

The teacher, we are told, 'avoids moralizing, criticising, giving values or evaluating. The adult excludes all hints of 'good' or 'right' or 'acceptable', or their opposites.' Sidney Simon, writing in the preface to <u>Meeting Yourself Halfway</u>, has an intriguing, almost evangelical belief in the liberation this approach can offer. "I sincerely believe that they (the exercises) can help you as they have so many others to meet your real self, a self grounded in reality, and flourishing in joy. It is a chance to be reborn again, and to soar as brightly as a shooting star'[11]. This sounds just like the material for reluctant learners on a Friday afternoon!!

By this view, values don't simply transmit, and they cannot be taught, but they can be learned through the process of clarification. Full values must meet all the seven criteria already mentioned, whilst anything that does not meet all seven, is not a value but a value-indicator, which, as might be imagined, indicates that a value is in the process of 'becoming'.

As a method of ME on the American/Canadian scene, it is most popular, even its critics agree upon that, but it has been described as 'amoral' or 'laissez-faire', with moral content giving way to a process without standards. The debate cannot of course be other than mentioned here, but my own position is that if a young person had nothing else except Values Clarification exercises then he would have a deficient grounding for his values. But this is hardly possible, because at every turn he will meet other sets of values pointing towards alternative authorities, with some claiming to be of ultimate significance. Any teacher wishing to examine in detail the case against values clarification should study a recent book <u>Yes, Virginia, There is Right and Wrong</u> by Kathleen M. Gow[12].

The strength of the Values Clarification approach is that it is useful in helping students to become aware of their own values. It has an important role to play in cautioning teachers against restrictive forms of ME: in presenting morality as a package deal. The choosing and cherishing as they touch upon human emotion are a very important aspect of moral education. They offer a great variety of activities that invite reflection and analysis. Some are in a real sense 'games', but not games that people play merely to kill time; rather they are tools of a serious but not necessarily solemn search. In a classroom they can be individual investigations, in fact some are so private that a student would want to see them as he would a private diary, for his eyes only. Others could well be shared with family or friends. The shared strategies are group-orientated because only a group interaction makes them meaningful. A typical 'elementary' exercise in values clarification might ask the student to rank activities, decisions or values in order of preference.

Example:- Which would you rather be?

(number your preferences 1 to 6, placing the number 1 next to your first choice, the number 2 next to your second choice and so on.)

.... an Olympic gold-medal winner

.... a diplomat for the United Nations

.... the discoverer of a cure for cancer

.... a rock music composer

.... the owner of a large shop

.... a priest, rabbi, or minister of religion.

Why would you want to be your number 1 choice?

What's important about the occupation you chose?

What might be important about the others?

Such activities attempt to direct the student's attention to some of the values behind their preferences, although initially there may be some problem in actually understanding what is meant by 'a value'. Lists and activities can begin in a simple fashion and move to become complex. I see no reason why a teacher who considers rational clarity, or moral imperatives to be more important cannot still use value clarification exercises in order to expose the process of valuing. There is a real danger of individual relativism, and the approach as it stands often fails to distinguish the fundamental difference between a moral and a non-moral question. But as is shown in the final part of this chapter the values - clarification method in conjunction with other approaches has a distinctive contribution to make.

The Moral Reasoning Approach

It might well be argued and easily supported that Lawrence Kohlberg is the leading researcher in the field of ME. In his work at the Center for Moral Development at Harvard he claims to have gone far beyond the limitations of the V/C method. His six, (or is it seven) stage cognitive development theory has been the subject of intense research and scrutiny over the past twenty-five years. If it is moral reasoning that a teacher wants to develop, then this must be the overarching framework to follow.

Drawing on Piaget and Dewey, he contends that an individual's thinking about moral situations matures according to a specific six-stage sequence.

Preconventional

(1)   Obedience and avoidance of punishment

(2)   Morality of personal interest

Conventional

(3)   Approval from authority - fixed rules

(4)   Maintaining the social order

Post-Conventional/Principled

(5)   Social contract - general rights

(6)   Self-chosen ethical principles of universality.

At its core, Kohlberg's theory assumes the existence of a positive force, a 'telos' that is capable of moving in the direction of more sophisticated and more comprehensive moral judgements. Through intensive interviewing Kohlberg came to the conclusion that all people move through these stages in invariant sequence, although any individual may stop at a particular stage. A young child is at Stage (1), and then most people move to Stage (2). As early as age nine but usually later most Americans enter Stage (3), and some of them pass into Stage (4) in the middle of adolescence. The transition to Stage (5) takes place if at all when people are in their late teens, or early twenties, or even later, and very few people attain Stage (6). Those who do are usually over thirty. The Seventh stage has been suggested as a mystical-cosmic stage of development.

The teacher's task then is to facilitate this natural impulse towards growth, with an environment (ideally like the Custer School) that supports and provokes the development, along with schemes of work that promote a cognitive conflict leading to a higher stage of moral reasoning.

The teacher interested in using Kohlberg's stages of moral reasoning will find ample material on his research, and detailed reaction by psychologists and philosophers, but very little on the British educational scene by way of classroom materials.

The typical stories or moral dilemmas used to stimulate discussion and promote development from one stage to the next, range from the familiar 'Heinz dilemma' which is about the morality of stealing a drug that could save a life, and is the standard one used in a moral judgement interview, to a series found in Selected Papers from Lawrence Kohlberg, with titles such as:-

Secluded country road

Dating outside your race

Drunken driving

A noisy child

In each case a brief story sets the scene, and presents a moral dilemma; the teacher's task is to probe the reasons given by the students for their moral judgements.

e.g. **Secluded country road**

A couple was walking on a secluded country road. Suddenly two boys on a motorcycle pulled up. They looked like members of a motorcycle gang, and appeared to be very tough. They told the boy 'Go and leave the girl to us. Nothing will happen to you if you leave but if you refuse we will kill you'.

1. What should the boy do, stay and fight and at least attempt to protect the girl? Or leave as he was told?

2. Is there a point at which a person's honour is more important than a life?

3. What if the girl was not a girlfriend but simply someone he knows only slightly?

4. Suppose while he was trying to decide what to do he became firmly convinced that the two boys would physically harm the girl, if he left. Before he thought that they were just talking tough, but now he is convinced that they are serious and will probably harm the girl if he leaves. Does this change his responsibility?

The discussion leader/teacher is quite at liberty to present dilemmas in a variety of forms; orally, written, by recordings, films or videotapes, or as role-playing exercises. Then his aim is to confront students with a level of reasoning, one stage above their present level. The insistent word is ... **WHY?** Understandably, some students can only stand so much probing with this word, and the leader's skill comes in knowing how much pressure to apply, and when to stop.

There is no reason why a teacher shouldn't develop such techniques for leading moral discussions, or for writing moral dilemmas to be used in social studies, R.E., or English. The skill is intuitive for some, but even so requires thoughtful application. The implications for significant changes in school democracy are beyond the scope of this chapter.

Schools Council Humanities Project (HCP)

This project, set up in 1967 under the directorship of Lawrence Stenhouse, differs from the previous schemes in that it was not designed as a ME programme. However, the aim, "to develop an understanding of social situations and human acts and of the controversial value issues they raise", clearly reveals its concern with values, emotions and reasoning.

Unlike Lifeline, in which the adolescents themselves selected the issues, the project team behind HCP selected materials that would be educationally worthwhile; human issues of universal concern. The Project proceeded on the basis that controversial issues should be handled in the classroom. Yet because they were controversial, there was no clear cut 'right' answer, or undivided attitude. The other major premises were that:-

(a) The teacher would submit his teaching in controversial areas to the criterion of neutrality, i.e. he would regard it as part of his responsibility not to promote his own views.

(b) The mode of enquiry in such areas should have discussion rather than instruction at its core.

(c) Divergence of view should be protected rather than consensus.

(d) The teacher as chairman should none the less have responsibility for the quality and standard of learning.

Material is supplied in packs which provide foundation collections in nine areas: War and Society, Education, The Family, Relationships between the Sexes, People and Work, Poverty, Law and Order, Living in Cities, and Race. The packs include newspaper cuttings, short stories, pictures, film material etc. Teachers and students can of course introduce their own materials, and it is vital that the teacher knows the contents of the pack so that if the discussion loses its way or its momentum, then something else can be selected to enrich or enliven the proceedings.

The project was originally intended for the group of students between fourteen and sixteen years of age, of average and below-average ability, but has proved to be suitable for the complete ability range.

The neutrality stance of the teacher in this method has created a controversy in its own right, quite apart from the actual materials considered. Of course it has built-in problems both for staff and students, but should not be regarded as an inflexible constraint. The younger pupils may need more of a 'given' personal viewpoint, and all students could claim a right to ask the 'real teacher' to stand up at some point in their shared enquiry. But to balance this the teacher needs to probe, and tease, and clarify, and act as the enabler of exploration before he says where he happens to stand, that is if he stands on any particular moral spot, or if he hasn't already revealed his personal persuasions unintentionally. To state a personal view too firmly and at too early a stage, could cause some to give up in their own thinking, and others to switch to an attack on him at a premature stage, thus failing to explore moral issues. Thus, once more, a teacher involved in ME finds himself back at a point of balance, discerning that there is a time to speak, and there is a time to refrain from speaking.

For anyone considering a ME course who wants ready-made material the HCP looks especially attractive, as it can be supplemented with extras from any source - the Guardian or the Sun - the local Quakers, or Roman Catholics, - the Islamic centre or teenage magazines.

Social Morality Council's National ME Centre

Any consideration of programmes and materials in ME must include an outline of this centre[13]. The plan is the establishment of a national development service, the first of its kind for ME in primary and secondary schools. Such development will be undertaken in cooperation with schools, parents, local authorities and colleges, and by Field Advisers working in selected areas. The national resource and information centre was opened at S.Martin's College, Lancaster, in September 1979 and the first Field Adviser appointed in January 1980.

Their publication, A Plan for ME in Schools, provides a detailed overview of current approaches, including a carefully considered rationale of underlying assumptions, moral and spiritual values, and the outline of a fresh approach to the development of ME in schools both primary and secondary.

It is quick to point out that this is not a project of limited duration, and is not in competition with other projects, some of which have been discussed so far in this chapter. Projects may be of interest to particular schools or particular staff, may be wedded to one particular theory or be regarded as yet another optional extra. This document says firmly that ME is not an optional extra, and it is here to stay. 'A vital factor in the planning of ME' should be a new partnership with R.E., with the potential sources of conflict between the two brought out into the open and defused before they undermine cooperation. This is a sound move.

It is intended tht the resources of this centre in terms of information and materials are to be made widely known and available, through a national network, occasional booklets, or periodicals, needed to complement the more academic Journal of Moral Education.

The S.M.C. sees ME as crossing all subject boundaries; all subjects have a dimension of values and meaning, including a moral element, implicit in their discipline and content, and schools neglect this to the loss of all. Dialogue with Examination Boards is also taking place which it is hoped will lead to the relevant modification of assessment procedures.

The 'Plan' which surely must be compulsory reading for any teachers considering ME, concludes with a realistic and constructive synthesis. "A value-free teacher would be like a colour-blind gardener. There should therefore be some attempt to reach a basic philosophy of ME. In our view its aim could be defined as the growth of children in two directions; towards (i) personal autonomy and (ii) towards human solidarity.

This dual principle, with the balance and tension it implies, is considered to be common ground for the religious and humanist traditions in this country, for both of which the two directions are not contradictory but complementary".

This is an intelligent attempt towards reconciliation. But it should be noted that balance implies just the correct amount of tension, and the very enthusiasm for moral education aroused by the plan could be sufficient to disturb the balance. However, overall the Social Morality Council's work is a sign of hope; there is a job to be done.

The preceding part of this chapter has all too briefly tried to outline some programmes and some approaches to ME. As the teacher now moves from theory to practice, so some of the classroom inter-actions mentioned at the outset begin to emerge; laughter and aggression, tension, perhaps tears and smiles, anger or sheer mystification. Background and antecedent factors react with materials and with adolescent personalities. In my experience none of the ME schemes really takes into consideration the great range of personality development in any one class, or the quite random mix of emotional maturity in a given group. Sometimes the shared ME exercise or discussion can be a profitable mix, whilst with another group of emerging personalities, the issues can produce a controversy that has much heat and very little light. I say 'apparently' because there is no scheme for analysis that can really account for the ingredients that account for 'growth'. A strangely assorted diet of human experiences moves us towards some semblance of maturity. Can more be said? Just how the total range of experiences, contrived, planned and accidental all come together in some integrated form is part of the mysterious delight of being human. We need to be suspicious of any over-tidy theory that dares to presume too much.

Methods (1)

Discussion

It is of course central, but all too often projects simply assume that students have the necessary skills to cope with controversial material. It can easily become a pooling of ignorance. Education into discussion is hard work, but I know of no other way for much of a ME course. The ability to listen, to reflect, to weigh up a case, and to speak to an idea rather than at a person, grow slowly. Small 'buzz' group discussion after perhaps seeing a film or listening to a speaker, helped by a guiding work-sheet through which all have something to do, can be a helpful device. So much depends on space and location.

Method (2)

Great use should be made of the community resources available to any school. By this I mean speakers (not necessarily experts) from local churches, and charities, pressure groups, almost anyone who has part of the human story to tell.

Method (3)

Apart from the range of commercially produced materials for ME, daily newspapers, a huge stack of them, and a wide range of magazines should be available. A particular mention should be made of the colour supplement magazines given with Sunday papers. Any teacher involved with ME would be well advised to be on good terms with local newsagents who will usually be pleased to provide free of charge spare copies of these supplements after the weekend.

Method (4)

At Burleigh College, Loughborough, a novel method was started in 1980 that enabled youngsters with learning difficulties to each have a 'Tutor-mother' living nearby in the local community. The scheme meant that for a day or so each week, the student would spend his or her time with a mother and her young children, in the home, sharing the routine, talking, working, and playing. It wasn't started with moral considerations as its main concern, but on the matter of relationships, or **EMP** and **PHIL** to use John Wilson's terms, it was moving in the realm of moral education.

Method (5)

Shared experiences

The ability to use the day-to-day experiences within the life of the school, touching students and staff, is of central importance to ME. There is a delicate balance here, whereby the teacher invites the students to 'talk about' what is happening in the life of the school and community. There is the risk of being subversive, and of probing too far but it has to be acknowledged and taken. In turn the staff member can happen to mention incidents, meetings, arguments, happy times and conflict happenings, all of which help to make ME live and be enjoyable, and at the same time be accountable in terms acceptable to Wilson, Kohlberg, the Lifeline project or the value-clarifiers. If these experiences can extend to field trips and residential courses, outside the normal curriculum, of course the sharing becomes richer, deeper and more spontaneous.

Method (6)

Examinations

To some, the very idea of an examination in this area would be dismissed as absurd, but I think the idea deserves more investigation. At one level, if the ME centre at Lancaster is 'in dialogue' with examination boards, and moral education is seen as implicit in all subjects, then this could in time be reflected in formal examination questions. This is already so in many of the personal/social aspects of Religious Studies, and Social Studies, and so long as the examination isn't pretending to produce a rank order of moral experts and moral idiots, it has an important part to play. Many aspects of ME lend themselves to appraisal, and the approach of the Farmington Trust with its correct use of language, and the relevant study of the facts should indicate the aspects of ME I have in mind.

Project work on human rights or prejudice, enquiries into violence or poverty, many of the areas explored by HCP, or imaginative schemes linked with community service could all be available for assessment. They would not presume to touch upon those softer and personal areas of concern in terms of measurement. That would be an offence, but such a study would be providing the enriched means of their possible development. By way of comparison, the study of moral philosophy or theology doesn't claim to make men moral or godly, but it equips them with a detailed and structured knowledge of the terrain, without which informed judgements would be difficult to make.

The syllabus 'Integrated Humanities' offered by JMB, with its wide range of topics and acceptable forms of teacher-assessed assignments, is worthy of consideration if a school is looking for an over-arching scheme for a common-core approach to moral enquiry.

In any programme of moral education there has to be space for individual personalities and group interaction to be expressed, and this implies a degree of freedom in the classroom. Once a group of adolescents has space of this kind, there can be no guarantee that it will be used to promote cognitive or affective moral development. It may well become the opportunity for confident teenager 'X' to pour scorn on shy 'Y'. This is quite simply a built-in factor, once education in this area of knowledge and experience is considered worthwhile. It needs therefore to be balanced by the fact that the teacher must remain the allocator and just controller of 'freedom', in the classroom world at least. He is, or should be after all, the moral expert, not in his deeds, but by virtue that he has an understanding of moral categories and moral reasoning; he knows the terrain.

The Newsom report reminded teachers that "they can only escape from their influence over the moral and spiritual development of their pupils by closing their doors". Despite the present cuts, this is not a realistic solution!! In fact the government support given to the SMC centre and the recommendation in Working papers by HM Inspectorate – Curriculum 11–16 indicate that a school without a carefully balanced programme of ME will be considered out of touch, and failing to meet the needs of young people.

An integration of ME programmes and approaches

The Lifeline project offers a seven point checklist for moral education. This list is supplemented below by reference to other projects and materials. Hopefully this is how in practice teachers might set about the task rather than following just one approach and excluding the rest.

Effective moral education should:-

	If Lifeline is taken as the basic programme it needs the following to achieve a total balanced approach
(1) Describe, if not define what is meant by 'moral'.	– Kohlberg's moral reasoning and Wilson's moral components
(2) Provide us with means of deciding what we ought to do in any inter-personal situation which puzzles us.	– Use of Values Clarification schemes and a consideration of Religious/Theistic claims (**)
(3) Itself be rationally supported or supportable.	– Use of Kohlberg and Wilson.
(4) Motivate us to behave morally.	– Kohlberg (as used in prison, see Collected Papers) (**) RE providing a vehicle for the visionary quality 'habitual vision of greatness' aspect. Plus HCP materials.
(5) Make it clear that morality is more than treating those well who treat us well.	– Probably all approaches have a contribution here.
(6) Underline the fact that moral behaviour is not simply a matter of accepting social norms, that it involves making personal decisions sometimes in conflict with such norms	– Definitely Kohlberg, plus Wilson's moral components. (Stress on concept of justice). Evidence perhaps from HCP/Lifeline to illustrate
(7) Be interesting and enjoyable	– An important ingredient but a fearsome counsel of perfection if expected at every stage.

(**) Religion and Morality, whilst certainly not identical, do need to be partners in secular education.

"Having in general terms pushed religion and morality apart, it is in my view time for us seriously to explore their relatedness . . . their functional relatedness, cognitively and emotionally. Religion is among other things a response to the universal, though suppressable human need for meaning structures which can be projected upon 'the whole show'. Moral principles and rules when adopted may well need to be placed in a wider context of meaning; the religious claims need at least to be examined."[14]

Notes

1 Barrow, R., Moral Philosophy for Education, George Allen and Unwin, 1975; Downey, M.E. and Kelly, A.V., Moral Education: theory and practice, Harper and Row, 1978; Harris, A.E., Teaching Morality and Religion, Allen and Unwin, 1976; Hersh, R.H., Miller, J.P., and Fielding, G.D., Models of Moral Education, Longman, 1980; Taylor, M.J., Policy and Progress In Moral Education, N.F.E.R., 1975.

2 Wilson, J., Practical Methods of Moral Education, Heinemann, 1972.

3 McPhail, P., Moral Education in the Secondary School, Longman, 1972.

4 McPhail, P., op.cit.

5 Wilson, J., 1972, op.cit. See also, Wilson, J., Williams N., and Sugarman, B., Introduction to Moral Education, Penguin, 1967; Wilson, J., A Teacher's Guide to Moral Education, Geoffrey Chapman, 1973.

6 Wilson, J., 1972, op.cit.

7 Wilson, J., Education in Religion and Emotions, Heinemann, 1971.

8 Wilson, J., 1972, op.cit.

9 Wilson, J., 1972, op.cit.

10 Simon, S.B., <u>Values Clarification: A Handbook</u>, Hart Public-
   ations, 1972, also his <u>Meeting Yourself Halfway</u>, Argus
   Communications, 1974; Raths, L.E., <u>Values and Teaching</u>,
   Merrill, 1966. See also Galbraith, R.E. and Jones, T.M., <u>Moral
   Reasoning - a Teaching Handbook for adapting Kohlberg to the
   classroom</u>, Greenhaven Press, 1976.

11 Simon, S.B., op.cit., p.57.

12 Gow, K.M., <u>Yes, Virginia, There is Right and Wrong</u>, John
   Wiley, 1980.

13 The Social Morality Council is based at 23 Kensington Square,
   London, W.8.; their useful publications include <u>A Plan for
   Moral Education in Schools</u> and <u>A Secondary School Resource
   Directory</u>; see also the linked work of the Moral Education
   Resource Centre, S. Martin's College, Lancaster, and in
   particular Gates, B., (ed.) <u>Religious Education Directory for
   England and Wales</u>, 1982.

14 Wright, D., Some thoughts on moral education, <u>Journal of Moral
   Education</u>, vol. 6, no. 1, 1976.